TOURIST SERVICE SATISFACTION

Francis P. Noe

SAGAMORE PUBLISHING

Champaign, Illinois
www.sagamorepub.com

©1999 Sagamore Publishing
All rights reserved.

Interior Layout: Michelle R. Dressen
Cover Design: Julie L. Denzer

ISBN:1-57167-390-3
Library of Congress Card Catalog Number: 99-62749

Printed in the United States of America.

■ Aim & Scope of Series

ADVANCES IN TOURISM APPLICATIONS provides a new forum for organizing and presenting emerging theory and management practices in five broadly defined areas of tourism management: (1) destination marketing, (2) destination management, (3) environment, (4) policy, and (5) statistics and theory. This new series of monographs attempts to fill an important gap between textbooks and journal articles, representing a comprehensive discussion of the most current theories and/or practices by leading scholars and industry professionals. Each volume identifies and discusses the most current theories and/or practices relevant to a specific topic, provides concrete examples and explanations of the importance of these theories/practices to the tourism industry, and provides extensive bibliographic resources.

As editors of the series, we want to encourage and facilitate the creativity of researchers and managers in tourism. Specifically, we invite readers to contribute by submitting manuscripts and/or case studies which describe innovative applications in the tourism industry. We welcome your ideas and suggestions for future topics and look forward to joining you on this journey of building knowledge for the 21st century.

· ·

Dr. Daniel R. Fesenmaier
Dept. of Leisure Studies
University of Illinois at
Urbana-Champaign
Champaign, IL USA

Dr. Joseph T. O'Leary
Dept. of Forestry &
Natural Resources
Purdue University
W. Lafayette, IN USA

Dr. Musaffer S. Uysal
Dept. of Hospitality and
Tourism Management
Virginia Polytechnic Institute
Blacksburg, VA USA

Other titles currently available in the
Advances in Tourism Applications Series

VOLUME ONE
Measuring Tourism Performance
Tzung-Cheng (T.C.) Huan and Joseph O'Leary

VOLUME TWO
Making Visitors Mindful: Principles for Creating Quality Sustainable Visitor Experiences Through Effective Communication
Gianna Moscardo

VOLUME THREE
Tourism Policy: The Next Millennium
David L. Edgell, Sr.

VOLUME FOUR
Positioning Tourist Destinations
Allen Z. Reich

VOLUME FIVE
Tourism Service Satisfaction
Francis P. Noe

. . . .

Upcoming titles

VOLUME SIX
Meta-Evaluation: Achieving Effective Tourism Marketing Programs
Arch G. Woodside and Marcia Y. Sakai

VOLUME SEVEN
Entrepreneurship and Innovation in Tourism
Sustainable Community Tourism Development
Thomas D. Potts

VOLUME EIGHT
Entrepreneurship and Innovation in Tourism
Frank Go

VOLUME NINE
The Design Analysis and Improvement of Tourist Services
Eric Laws

VOLUME TEN
Tourism Destination Marketing: Organizations, Strategies, and Programs
Alastair Morrison

*As long as you want to achieve,
you are alive—but if you are
satisfied—you are dead.*

Joseph Conrad, 1913-1985

Contents

CHAPTER FOUR
Attribute Indicators and Specifying Satisfaction

CHAPTER FIVE
Measurement of Tourism Satisfaction

■ Preface

THIS REVIEW of satisfaction studies and research is the outcome of my work in attempting to understand public responses to facilities, services, and programs offered to tourists by the U.S. National Park Service. Prompted by inquiries of park managers about how they could do a "better job of servicing the public," research into program evaluation methods led me to examine a number of approaches that all converged around the question of how to represent satisfaction or dissatisfaction in a reliable, valid, parsimonious, predictable, and communicable scientific manner. Readers will recognize these principles as the tenets of science.

The foundation of this research benefited from an effort begun in the Southeast Regional Office in the late 1970s by such notable stalwarts as the former Director of the National Park Service, Gary Everhardt, currently superintendent of the Blue Ridge Parkway. In commenting on the public use of parks, he stated that "we need to be more sensitive to the needs of the public and how we can better accommodate them without destroying the very thing that they came to experience—the nature of the park. If national parks are here to serve the public, we ought to know how the public thinks, feels, and acts toward what we plan and develop for them" (Jurowski et al., 1995-6, p. 48). Others, such as the Deputy Director of the Southeast Region, Neal Guse, and the Regional Chief Scientist at that time, Dr. Jay Gogue, also provided support and encouragement. That was a time when scientific research set the standard for credibility, and management's input helped develop an applied perspective. Because the National Park Service programs were modest, the agency sought assistance from outside researchers largely at universities, who through competitive contracts or basic agreements provided the field results, reports, and research findings. This approach occurred long before it became fashionable for those in Federal Government to talk about partnerships and empowerment. As a result, that competitive spirit produced some outstanding findings. Those most deserving of recognition are professors and researchers such as: Adrian Aveni, William Hammitt, John D. Hutcheson, William Little, Carey McDonald, Robert Snow, Claudia Jurowski, Muzaffer Uysal, Myron Floyd, Charles Burchell, and most important the park service superintendents and their staffs in the Southeast Region whose cooperative spirit made the field work and on-site sampling a success in each and every project. You might suspect that I am very proud of what the National Park Service represents, and you are correct. There is a singular word in the agency's name that says it all and what this book is about—Service. From day one, I was fortunate to experience a sincere and caring manner about how Park Service personnel look after the nation's parks and the touring public. I would not trade that experience for anything. But the lessons do not stop there, for others also lead with a spirit of service and care.

During a recent trip, while waiting for a scheduled departure at Atlanta's Hartsfield airport, I met a very gracious, unassuming, and friendly individual by the name of Larry P. Castellani. We briefly discussed this book that I was editing at the time. He told me that he attended the Disney University, which is no Mickey Mouse of customer service, and shared his views on service. When leaving, he gave me his business card, whereupon I first learned that he was the President and Chief Executive Officer of Tops Markets Inc. What I learned from him should be a lesson for all tourist providers, namely that "the front line is the bottom line." When new markets were brought on line, Larry put on an apron, stocked shelves, and greeted the customer. And did the public take notice? You bet they did. Many were quick to point out that he was in the "front line serving." When you stop to think about it, most of us live on the "front line," and it sure feels good to know that the people at the top appreciate you. This CEO has recently been promoted in the Royal Ahold firm, the Dutch holding company of Tops Markets, to work on expanding markets in China, Thailand, Singapore, Malaysia, and Indonesia, I suspect in part because of a strong service orientation. I also suspect that his sensitivity to the customer began in 1962 when he began his work career by first stocking shelves and interacting with customers, where you quickly learn that service to the customer takes priority because you are on the "front line."

In the hospitality business, J. Willard Marriott, Sr., or Bill, stands out in my mind as a prophet of service who knows what working the front line meant. Beginning in 1927 with A&W Root Beer and Hot Shoppes in food service in Washington, D.C., Bill Marriott later added the first of many Motor Hotels in Arlington, Va., beginning with the Twin Bridges. He catered to America's spirit of mobility by serving the growing needs of the driving and flying public. Built on a value system or foundation of family, hard work, God, and country, that initiative led to one of today's leading hospitality companies with more than 4,700 units serving more than four million customers a day. Those pillars of personal value were tied together by the "golden rule." It took more than Bill, his wife Allie, brothers, and sons to build Marriott International. It took satisfied employees or the internal customer. That is the other side of the coin in building a loyal customer base. In 1997, Fortune Magazine named Marriott International one of the 100 best companies to work for in America. On the night before Bill Jr. would be appointed executive vice-president, Bill Sr. in a letter to his son laid down fifteen "guideposts" for his consideration. Of those, six are directly related to the internal customer: "(1) People are No. 1—their development, loyalty, interest, team spirit. Develop managers in every area. This is your prime responsibility. (2) Don't criticize people but make a fair appraisal of their qualifications with their supervisor only (or someone assigned to do this). Remember, anything you say about someone may (and usually does) get back to them. There are few secrets. (3) See the good in people and try to develop those qualities. (4) Don't try to do an employee's job for him—counsel and suggest.

(5) Inefficiency: If it cannot be overcome and an employee is obviously incapable of the job, find a job he can do or terminate now. Don't wait. (6) Think objectively and keep a sense of humor. Make the business fun for you and others" (O'Brien, 1977, pp. 266-267). Sound advice for nurturing a satisfied employee who in turn nurtures a satisfied customer.

To be successful in providing satisfaction, it takes more than having just satisfied employees and customers; it takes another kind of vision of knowing where the two can meet to be happy. Another CEO and founder of a diversified lending company, C. Paul Sandifur, Sr., of Metropolitan Mortgage and Securities Inc. of Spokane, Wash. is worth taking note of because of his unique perspective. As a dealer and holding company of property, he took chances and developed real estate holdings that included a resort on one of the smaller Hawaiian Islands long before it became a popular destination. Eventually, it proved a success. As part of his autobiography, he confidently predicts that "in the future we will be blessed with so much leisure time, that new and developing industries will be mainly for travel, entertainment, and pleasure" (Sandifur, 1995, p. 113). That truly seems to be the case in today's global economy. We must be prepared to service, entertain, and care for the tourist. In the end, satisfaction or its alternative dissatisfaction is all that hangs in the balance. The choice is clear; resources must be geared toward maximizing satisfaction and minimizing dissatisfaction so that opportunity will not be lost as today's world embraces tourism.

Francis P. Noe

Atlanta, Georgia
February, 1999

■ Introduction

N O GREATER CHALLENGE exists in the marketplace than for a business to be responsible for providing satisfactory tourist and hospitality services. The tourist chooses to travel not out of duty or responsibility, but out of a personal, discretionary choice in leisure time. The tourist is not bound to satisfy any mandatory institutional prerequisites to travel. The tourist is not accountable to any societal organizations that he or she particularly needs to satisfy. The tourist is not bound to seek satisfaction from a limited set of choices. In the end, tourists simply expect to satisfy themselves through the services that are available to them during leisure time.

Three main research strategies are followed to achieve an understanding of tourist perceptions of satisfaction. The first exploits the literature on service quality and satisfaction from the business perspective. Many researchers and consultants have made it their primary goal to focus on issues and problems of customer satisfaction. Many of the lessons learned from the business perspective of these experts are valuable indicators of what produces service satisfaction. For a tourist professional, many of these lessons may be applicable in a tourist and hospitality situation. Because many of these lessons are based on the quantitative results of marketing surveys, they command even greater attention. A review of this literature with special attention focused on organizations directly involved in tourism are selected as models of how some companies deal with customer satisfaction.

A second strategy focuses inquiry more specifically on the hotel, hospitality, restaurant, recreation, and transportation sectors of tourism that are continually refining methods for keeping, finding, and satisfying customers. In the United States, travel and tourism is either the third or fourth largest industry in America, depending how you calculate that market impact. It is not an insignificant part of the economy. As an integral part of this strategy, the closely associated field of leisure-recreation studies, of which travel plays a major role, is also included in this review because of the past interest in the subject of customer evaluation and satisfaction. Also, many of the primary or secondary interests of a traveler are associated with some kind of leisure activity, be it a sport, hobby, sightseeing, or just rest and relaxation.

The third and final strategy takes an analytic empirical perspective that places the weight of any understanding of what affects tourist hospitality satisfaction on a platform of quantitative or qualitative evidence. Conclusions reached are based on research and surveys data as much as possible. In other words, the voice of the customers, what they perceive, believe, judge, and feel about a satisfactory experience, underpins this review. Statistical data and interpretation form the basis for making judgments about customer satisfaction. As a matter of principle, the findings of the researchers are scientifically neutral, objectively unbiased, and do not put words in the mouth of the customer. More precise case studies using a satisfaction model illustrate how it is possible to begin to understand more about how to treat attributes that may affect a travel experience.

The overriding purpose of this work is to present an applied perspective on customer satisfaction for the tourist provider or student, and not simply another examinant treatise. Two types of social attributes guide this research toward a practical application. Some attributes diagnose a tourist's response to service, while other attributes explain or predict differences in a tourist's perception of satisfaction.

It is inescapable, but specific attributes must be the object of analysis in dealing with the tourist process. Facility, service, program, and personnel attributes are subject to questioning and inspection by the tourist customer. These attributes are specific program ingredients perceived by some measure of customer satisfaction. An understanding and treatment of tourist attributes plays an important step in understanding, managing, and measuring satisfaction.

■ 1

Significance of Satisfaction

WHY SATISFACTION AND TOURISM?

Reasons for Tourism Satisfaction

THE SIGNIFICANCE of examining tourist perceptions of satisfaction is important for understanding what positively influences the travel experience. A principal function of the hotel, hospitality, and tourist industry is organized around satisfying the client. When the tourist is satisfied, then the travel services are credited with providing effective service opportunities. What affects the outcome of a satisfactory service and what is known about providing satisfactory services are fundamental questions defining the principal scope of this inquiry. But first, this chapter explores how the satisfaction model came to be defined.

The rationale for linking tourism and satisfaction seems hardly a debatable point, but there are many different sides to satisfaction during a travel experience that need elaboration. It is not a simple singular distinction. A popular textbook on tourism by McIntoch, Goeldner, and Ritchie (1995, p. 9) defines the very role of being a tourist as seeking "various psychic and physical experiences and satisfactions." Given this perspective, it would be very easy to confuse seeking satisfaction in travel with a motivation for traveling when in fact, that is only part of the explanation. Traveling for pleasure may be the result of numerous push-pull motivations resulting from needs, drives, or value orientations. The resulting satisfaction of actually fulfilling such motivations does not exist in the abstract. It is almost always identified with a particular travel destination for a chosen trip. Travel motivation "research represents a summary of travel satisfaction for a particular destination. It is thus not a pure or clean analysis of travel motivation but helps us to understand the importance of travel motivation in tourism studies by emphasizing that for travel motivation to be useful and meaningful, it must be put in a context" (McIntoch et al., 1995, p. 171). The previous quotation was taken from Chapter 9, "Pleasure

Travel Motivation" prepared by Philip Pearce. And many specific contexts are presently being managed by tourism professionals that represent the lure and attraction of those "alien places and people, natural wonders, and the monuments and places of worship of ancient and alien civilizations that are among our most easily accessible sources of stimulus satisfaction" (Scitovsky, 1992, p. 280). In seeking this kind of satisfaction, Hanan and Karp (1989, pp. 166-167) predict that travel and entertainment will continue to offer opportunities for increased satisfaction through the 1990s as they become more intertwined. "Travel will become more convenient, affordable, and acceptable, and will undoubtedly rank high among beneficial forms of entertainment." Greater mobility and increasing business ties between nations predispose the public to greater acceptance of travel options. International unrest and environmental degradation is seen as a threat to travel progress and growth. But the world today, as it nears the turn of the century, is less prone to superpower conflict, although many regions are still rife with civil, ethnic, religious, or local armed warfare. Despite these sporadic conflicts, many more places are now open for business and organized to satisfy the tourist customer. The environment, especially national parks and preserves, is under great pressure from resource development. Increases in ecotourism and outdoor recreation are placing greater pressure on these national treasures. For the tourist professional and conservationist, this will remain an ongoing problem of accommodation to balance preservation interests together with travel desires. The problems are not insurmountable, but they will require compromise to insure that the public interests are served. There is too much to be gained to ignore the growing interest in ecotourism and travel.

The satisfying experiences that travel and vacationing potentially offer the consumer also produce reciprocal rewards and benefits for the tourist provider when satisfaction is successfully delivered. An example from the hospitality sector clearly demonstrates positive effects all can understand. Schneider and Bowen (1995, p. 11) report the results of a panel study of a restaurant chain demonstrating a correlation between customer satisfaction on day one and profits nine months later. Obviously, satisfaction counts for something, namely profit. In a free-enterprise system, profit motivates a business to grow. "Customer satisfaction is of interest to business only when it leads to profit: . . . by increasing the chances for repeat purchase. . . . It creates positive word-of-mouth promotion," increases "expenditure on current purchases," and positively "affects cash flow" (Barsky, 1995, p. 5). In short, "satisfying customers is the single best strategy a business can follow to make money" (Barsky, 1995, p. 6).

If travel and vacationing are inherently predisposed to provide satisfaction because of the nature of the activity, and if tourists are willing to pay for this service, then where could there possibly be a problem? It would seem that this is an ideal service situation both for the customer and tourist professional. "Vacationing is probably the most clearly stimulating form of recreation. Whether as an occasion for sightseeing . . . vacations are clearly a source of stimulation in the truest and best sense of the term" (Scitovsky, 1992, pp. 191-192). But there are discomfort costs associated with vacationing, i.e., "the noise of hotel rooms, the discomfort of unfamiliar beds and baths, the hazards of restaurant food, the crowding of resorts and beaches, the vagaries of the weather, or a reservation not being honored which some people are unwilling to undergo" (Scitovsky, 1992, p. 138). This is not an ideal situation. There are real downside problems and some, like the weather, are not manageable. A customer also wants price, quality, and service in good measure. To provide a tourist service, client satisfaction is essential. Satisfaction is the linchpin between a customer's motivations and a destination resort's profit. In real terms, the success or failure of tourism assets (transport, restaurants, hotels, host community) are evaluated subjectively on the client's own personal satisfaction scale. The resulting experience and attitude of the customer translates into future action or inaction. That is why understanding the nature of satisfaction is so important: because it is the bottom line both economically and personally.

CONCEPTUAL BASES FOR UNDERSTANDING SATISFACTION

Baseline Consensus Established

In 1977, a seminal effort was undertaken to provide a clear foundation for the study of satisfaction. Through a grant from the National Science Foundation and the sponsorship of the Marketing Science Institute, Hunt (1977b, pp. 1-2) organized a first-of-its-kind conference that was an important catalyst.

> **S**atisfaction shares a common evaluative connection between the attitude and act.

A major goal of the meeting was to speed up progress toward understanding satisfaction in marketing and overcome the lack of "cross-fertilization" of ideas between interested parties. Although it may be a basic tenet and function of business to satisfy a consumer's needs, the conference recognized that measures of satisfaction were still at an elementary level of development. Much of this early consolidation focused on conceptualization and measurement. Essentially, the work of the conference split into two concerns, those relating to conceptual approaches to satisfaction and others focusing on techniques or methods of measurement (Hunt, 1977a). Much has been accomplished since that time, but today, both concerns are still essential toward developing a complete analytic model.

Definitions of satisfaction varied slightly or emphasized different aspects. For the most part, however, no common conceptual consensus existed that clearly defined satisfaction. The essence of satisfaction was fundamentally identified more as a consumer concept or orientation containing a number of interrelated behavioral concepts. According to Czepiel and Rosenberg (1977, p. 93), "consumer satisfaction is an attitude in the sense that it is an evaluative orientation that can be measured." As a special kind of attitude it contains both a cognitive and affective component that tourist-customers will experience and express through their intentions and behavior. The attitude is a result of an evaluative process in which the social costs and benefits of a travel experience are weighed during and after the experience. In that sense, "it is a special kind of attitude because by definition it cannot exist prior to the purchase or consumption of the attitude object" (Czepiel and Rosenberg, 1977, p. 93). The resulting judgment is especially relevant for future use of a tourist destination. Tourist-customers may not have immediate plans to revisit a destination any time soon, but what they say through word-of-mouth to their friends, family, colleagues, and neighbors about how satisfied or dissatisfied they were with their experiences has consequences for future business. That decision may also have a residual bearing on how they feel about a booking agent, tour operator, rental car, lodging operators, and the host of services supporting that travel decision. The opportunity of enjoying a satisfactory travel experience is directly related to specific service offerings and how the consumer receives them. However, an attitude is more general and pervasive than a consumption experience, but satisfaction shares a common evaluative connection.

Another key definitional element of the satisfaction process was singled out by Miller (1977, pp. 72-73), who focused on the decision-making process that connected satisfaction to additional behavioral concepts. Miller proposes that "consumer satisfaction results from the interaction of levels of (a) expectations about anticipated performance and (b) evaluations of perceived performance" that are compared by the tourist to determine if the perceived performance met or exceeded expectations resulting in satisfaction. The perception process involves evaluating preconceived expectations about a tourist experience with the actual experience. It is a subjective process with the tourist-customer exercising control over the outcome through selective perception, rationalization, dissonance reduction, and face-to-face discussions with fellow travelers and service providers. As a result of this dynamic communication process, the tourist-customer seeks to reach a decision. Both expectations and perceptions of service performance underpin that decision process and shape its outcome. Responses of satisfaction are neither static nor fixed attitudes. Neither are expectations that are constantly being retested against real experiences. That is why it is important for tourist providers to continually test their market for new and emerging interests and trends. Consumer interests are most subject to change in a competitive market, so it stands to reason that tourist providers must remain open and flexible to new and different innovative ideas.

If the above aspects of a satisfaction definition are pieced together, satisfaction is conceived as stepping away from an experience and evaluating it (Hunt, 1977a,b). Satisfaction is separated from more emotionally charged responses. Sentiments and emotions are part of the process, but they contribute just as other psychographic and lifestyle dispositions influence an evaluative judgment. Satisfaction includes emotional evaluation. Consider judgments of satisfaction as a kind of sanitized response without actual, behavioral-emotional manifestations but influenced by them. Satisfaction is more synonymous with a state of acceptability. The converse, dissatisfaction, remains more akin to a form of unacceptability.

Satisfaction does not take place in a social vacuum. Personal situations also influence how a tourist-customer achieves satisfaction. Society and culture in this modern world are linked together by mass transportation and communication offering a wide range of choices and options for the tourist-customer in a free market system. Withey (1977, p. 127) cites a number of empirical studies that suggest "judgments of satisfaction are more relative than absolute." The exposure of some customers to travel options may be almost limitless, whereas others are more narrowly confined to a limited situation. Specific kinds of travel satisfaction are judged in relative comparison to other kinds of vacation or holiday free-time situations. The relative importance of those decisions will vary by expectations and personal preference depending upon the significance assigned to them by the traveler. Recognizing the personal situation of available options comes closest to the true meaning of the maxim that the customer is always right when judging his relative situation. Differences in judgments inevitably vary across travel options. As in most decisions, comparisons are not only judged relative to each other, but are also personally weighted and valued given other choices about how to spend that discretionary amount of time.

A consumer's rate of consumption may also enter into the equation affecting satisfaction. This rate includes the pattern and volume of transactions made by the consumer. A higher number of transactions may sensitize or jade the tourist-customer. Hughes (1977) finds that dissatisfied and complaining consumers are more active purchasers. Dissatisfied customers also tend to purchase at a lower price, perhaps sacrificing quality but not their standards. The increased volume in transactions creates a larger experience pool for the consumer to draw upon, thereby refining and shaping comparisons. Because they may also seek out lower prices, they potentially take higher risks in compromising quality. As a result, high-volume travel customers may be more critical about their purchases. Such a condition may exist among high-volume tourists.

In review, the 1977 conference consolidated and provided a baseline of analytical thinking about how to theoretically conceptualize consumer satisfaction. Since that time, social science and marketing research have built on those earlier premises and foundations. A number of trends emerged as consequences. First, satisfaction is defined as a special kind of attitude because of the consumer's evaluative orientations resulting from the experience. More will be said about how this has been translated in today's working models in the next section. Second, satisfaction is a subjective judgment that is the result of the perceived discrepancy between what the customer expects and the actual experience with a service. The gap or difference between the two—the expectations and perception—comprise the basic structure of the model. Third, consumer satisfaction is also associated with emotions. Although the emotional commitment in a consumer situation is more controlled, that does not mean it is any less intense. Unlike many other situations, customers have avenues to vent their emotions in order to secure justice. Fourth, a judgment of satisfaction, either acceptable or unacceptable, is a relative act that is affected by the customer's past experience and exposure, training and status, and other exogenous variables which are part of today's still-evolving model. Essentially, an understanding of customer satisfaction has been built on a platform that is still being refined conceptually and empirically.

Current Definitional Consensus

A shift or change has occurred in the understanding of satisfaction, which questions its fundamental premise as a special attitude. In the 1920s, however, the answer was unambiguous. Social psychology was changing from a single, unscientifically based examination of instincts as the foundation for human interaction to a study of man's social situation and attitudes. It was then that the pioneering work of Allport (1924, pp. 407-410) recognized that the "good name or prestige of a business firm, though usually thought of as an attribute of the firm itself, is really an attitude common to a large number of patrons and citizens." He pointed out that this is a marketable asset and represents the readiness of a company to deal from a position of economic prestige. If over time, a company builds a record of public goodwill through "careful advertising and honest dealings," it will prosper. Today's business perspective is much the same despite changes from a more product-to-service oriented business climate. But consumer satisfaction is simply not another attitude. "Existing evidence tends to suggest that consumer satisfaction is different from, though similar or related to, other concepts such as attitudes" (Yi, 1990, p. 76).

The major emphasis in the business literature is much the same today as it was when Allport was writing about the good name of a business. According to Hanan and Karp (1989, p. 23), "Customer satisfaction is not a remedial strategy. It should be installed as the very genesis of a business." As the central focus of a business, "satisfaction is defined as a customer's perception of a single service experience, whereas quality is the accumulation of the satisfaction for many customers over many service experiences." Such post-evaluative experiences perhaps lead over time to a more general attitude. Moreover, service is equal to the perception of a "single" service as received and measured against the expected service received. The difference in the degree, direction, and discrepancy between the "perceptions" and "expectations" of a customer result in a level of satisfaction or dissatisfaction (Hill, 1992, pp. 44-47). This perspective essentially forms what is commonly referred to as a gap or discrepancy model that is still taking shape in current marketing research.

The gap model contains a minimum of two or sometimes three key concepts. Satisfaction and quality service are often treated together as functions of a customer's perceptions and expectations. The simplest model is the two-concept equation defined as $Q = P - E$. There are exceptions within this model. A zone of indifference exists among some customers who have not formed an expectation or do not care about a service. But for the most part, when perceptions (P) are equal to expectations (E), service quality (Q) is satisfactory. If expectations are higher than actual perceptions, a customer's rating becomes negative (Cottle, 1990, pp. 22-23). To improve customer satisfaction you either raise customer perceptions, lower their expectations, or both. Since an expectation is nothing more than an anticipation of receiving something favorable or acceptable, it is essential for any service company to develop realistic expectations among their customers. But "expectations and perceptions are factors that are hard to control" (Davidow and Uttal, 1989, p. 19).

They are difficult to control because perceptions and attitudes are subjective responses. They are heavily influenced by the ongoing personal situations that individuals are exposed to, and by competing opportunities that are as much ignored or overlooked given the dynamics of human interaction. Media and advertising techniques described in the next section are used not so much to mold as to control expectations.

In a three-concept model, the key elements remain the same as stated above. Customer satisfaction is determined by defining customer perceptions of quality, expectations, and preferences (Barsky, 1995, Ch. 2). Said another way, "satisfaction, or lack of it, is the difference between how a customer expects to be treated and how he or she perceives being treated" (Davidow and Uttal., 1989, p. 19). Customer satisfaction is created by exceeding expectations, delivering quality, and targeting customer preferences (Barsky, 1995, p. 66). Conceptualizing this process in quantitative terms, expectations are hypothetically measured from zero to exceed. Preferences are measured from most to least preferred for a specific service, while the perceived quality of service is measured by most to least valued. Because service quality and the concept of measurement are so important, both will be treated in separate chapters.

Understanding Expectations

Reaching back again historically to the 1920s, the molding and shaping of attitudes and expectations is recognized as an important business technique in dealing with potential customers. The following excerpt from its time is interesting in two ways. First, it illustrates that recreational taste is open to manipulation, as is the tourism recreation business today. Second, the recreation and entertainment business is criticized for what publishers and producers are offering for mass public consumption, a criticism still heard in our time. By controlling public opinion or expectations, Allport (1924, p. 410) observes that "as long as the tired seeker of recreation can be diverted by the vulgar humor of vaudeville, the covert sexuality of the farce, or the open sex appeal of the burlesque, and as long as he can identify himself with the luxury of the social life he envies on the cinematography screen, he will have little incentive for learning to enjoy true aesthetic appeals conveyed through the same media." These are harsh words for the simple pleasures of the working classes, but recognition of the power of advertising in the newspapers to shape public expectations. The producers of that kind of recreation, however, probably accurately reflected the true market expectations. These diversions were not appealing to the upper classes educated in the fine arts but sought largely by the blue-collar, male, working class. This example nicely illustrates the problem of fixing and establishing expectation levels for a market. Understanding a

> **C**ustomer satisfaction is created by exceeding expectations, delivering quality, and targeting customer preferences.

customer's level of perceived expectation is essential for a company in "establishing a fixed level."

According to Barsky (1995, pp. 26, 189), "expectation levels should be set high enough to attract business but accurate enough to reflect the reality of what is likely to be delivered 100 percent of the time." Misleading information or exaggerated promises can quickly erode good quality service. A customer's expectation is ultimately tested in a real situation by making judgments based on self-perceptions. In reality, customer expectations are an internalized set of standards that are applied in service situations. "Expectations are important because quality is a judgment against some standard." The perception of a service is judged to possess a degree of quality and those perceptions are judged in the context of a customer's expectations. To be successful in providing tourist services the perceptions of quality need to be "superior to the competition" (Schneider and Bowen, 1995, pp. 22-23). In essence, there is no harder standard for a company to meet.

The idea of expectations and manipulation of them progresses upon a foundation built on customer input. Customer expectations are defined by synthesizing outside cues about a service. Such cues emerge from the pre-decision, the decision, and post-decision process of consumption. "Expectations, like first impressions, are easily created and may last a long time. That is why knowing what creates initial expectations or what can affect expectations over time is so important to companies" (Barsky, 1995, pp. 20-21). However, ignoring those expectations, even if they do not apply to your service orientation, can be costly. For example, most hotel properties serving business and tourism in downtown San Francisco since 1990 are luxury establishments. While the renovation of the entrance to one of the older properties projected a new luxury level of service, its restaurant and coffee shop delivered third-rate service. The hotel never intended itself to be a luxury first-class establishment, but was so defined by the adjacent properties and upgraded entrance. As a result, management had to upgrade its service in the lobby and shops despite the lower rates it charged (Barsky, 1995). Customers judge their satisfaction/dissatisfaction against an expectation norm that they have created or that was established for them (Lele and Sheth, 1991, p. 139). Many companies try to compensate for poor service by thinking that a lower price alone will make everything better. It doesn't. They obfuscate by labeling a service as "economy first class" thereby confusing expectations. They plan service for the average when they ought to be looking at what the more demanding want. While it is unfortunate for that hotel in San Francisco, this situation perhaps could have been avoided if management identified more with their customer than the high-end market neighbors. But management has to trust that "understanding your customers' expectations and making the appropriate changes to improve satisfaction is possible only if you first 'listen' to what your customers say and then move quickly to act upon their suggestions. Listen as if you were an objective outsider" (Hinton and Schaeffer, 1994, p. 28). The ability to listen and learn from the customer is essential to an effective service program. Cottle (1990, pp. 22-23) recommends listening empathetically to your customer, which means putting yourself in the place of the customer. This sounds easy, but in practice it is very difficult to personally implement since a service person must resist speaking and offering conclusions. A passive-receptive role that conveys an openness to a customer's needs takes actions, not words. By directing questioning to obtain more specific and detailed information to help pinpoint the specific content of a customer's expectations, a service can be targeted to meet that request and actions planned to meet those ends.

Companies or organizations have initial choices to make in dealing with expectations in that they must choose a market and then a market segment, and also work to identify that market segment's expectations. The Kimco Hotel and Restaurant Co. was picked as an example by Schneider and Bowen (1995, pp. 43-44, 50) of how to successfully target a client group by using customer satisfaction data as a strategy for improvement. They found by buying older, run-down, historic buildings and converting them to charming "antique" style properties that offer affordable, "understated elegance and good food, there was a market." They provide a "perception of reality, not reality itself." They design facsimiles of interiors, not necessarily historically correct but what customers "think" they should look like. Most important, they sell "sleep," not meeting rooms or entertainment facilities. As such, they create value because expectations are exceeded at a fair price. It is important that each tourist "service must identify for itself the content and the form of customers expectations—that is, what the expectations are and the specific form the expectations take," and also determine the level of "importance" or value they connote for the customer (Schneider and Bowen, 1995, p. 26). Expectations are about concrete attributes of a service experience, but they must be identified in order to evaluate them. Naumann (1995, p. 104) indicates three attributes that are so general in nature that they are easily adaptable to tourism or hospitality service.

(1) "Search attributes" defined as service elements can be evaluated prior to purchase, such as a restaurant's star rating in the Mobil Travel Guide. Such attributes must accurately match or exceed customer expectations. Barsky (1995, p. 7) reports the attempts of one foreign airline to increase Japanese patronage by promising and delivering on big promises of fancy Japanese cuisine. The approach failed to satisfy that foreign market because the Japanese traveler rewards efficiency and value in an airline, not fine cuisine.

(2) "Experience-based attributes" are involved in actually evaluating the immediate experience of a restaurant meal or tourist service. Hotel customers are very "hypersensitive" to cues about service; staff uniforms, an orderly lobby, a paper strip on the commode, and complimentary beverages are examples of practices that can influence expectation levels within an ongoing experience (Davidow and Uttal, 1989, pp. 82-83).

(3) "Credence-based attributes" are experienced over an extended time by the customer who eventually forms a trusted opinion of a service. The Marriott Residence Inn, for example, established a level of public expectation through a credo stating that its staff will exceed the expectations of every guest, every day, every stay. How best to affect that expectation is a practical matter imple-

mented through daily customer relations. As a result, the Marriott Residence Inns consistently lead in market share (Naumann, 1995, p. 194).

Given a similar theme, the Holiday Crowne Hotels, an upscale plaza chain, is launching a new approach to attract and build guest loyalty. "Get to know us; we'll get to know you," is communicated through an advertising campaign. To help fulfil that goal, internal organizational changes are being adopted to help implement, track, and profile customer preferences for such things as pillows, snacks, and services individually tailored to their guest preferences (Rauscher, 1997a, p. 78). Similar programs exist at the Four Seasons Hotels and Resorts that track guest preferences for amenities, while the Inter-Continental's guest-recognition program tracks spending on hotel services: valet, laundry, concierge, and other services. As an approach to building guest credence, the Ritz-Carlton Repeat Guest History Program is held up as an industry standard for directing preferences to the appropriate staff upon booking a repeat stay (Barsky, 1995, pp. 139-143). In that program, the Ritz-Carlton Hotels, a Malcolm Baldrige Quality award winner with a Mobil five star rating, has established a "Gold standard" that concentrates on a guest's care and comfort, seeks to enliven the senses, promotes the well-being, and even "fulfills the unexpressed wishes and needs of our guests." As serving "ladies and gentlemen," its service posture is practiced by all employees who set very high uncompromising standards (Barsky, 1995, pp. 15, 33-35, 38, 112-113). Because the market niche at the Ritz Carlton is finely honed by management, no universal, automatic, customer expectation can be assumed for each service situation. Customers do not equally value the same attributes, so a value profile "requires that a firm really understand what attributes are important to each market segment, niche, or customer group" (Naumann, 1995, pp. 108-109), and then personalize the service to a guest. In order to further refine and target expectations, the idea of "mass customization" plays an important role in promoting a service by adding or deleting options that could introduce needed flexibility to tailor a service within a larger program of offerings. A kind of *a la carte* approach to satisfying customers is designed, and a way of personalizing those sought-after attributes is developed. Customization is found to be "more central to customers' expectations and perceptions of quality than reliability." It is not that reliability is not significant, but rather customization is more important for influencing perceived quality in the service than the product sector. Rather than trying to increase satisfaction by totally emphasizing the reliability of a service, it is better to recognize that there are reliability limits and shift attempts at better tailoring services to meet customer needs (Fornell, Johnson, Anderson, Cha, and Bryant, 1996, p. 14). But do not attempt customizing services without sufficient staff; "a downsized firms' future financial performance will suffer if repeat business is dependent on labor intensive customized service" (Fornell et al., 1996, p. 7).

In the case of the above hotel programs, they are designed to build credence in a personalized service tailored to a guest who shares a market niche with others of near-similar taste and expectations. Basically, the customer defines what attributes are important from a range of options, and the service organization functions within their schedule to deliver them.

Expectation Strategies

Successful companies manage customer expectations by controlling their advertising and communications. They also choose managers, agents, and intermediaries to set correct expectations. They prefer to underpromise by positioning themselves to be perceived as delivering more than what is expected (Lele and Sheth, 1991, p. 65). Delivering credible communication that keeps expectations in check is a manageable strategy. Understating a service allows for pleasant surprises and gives an opportunity to the tourist provider to adjust service if problems arise. Because a condition exists that "clients actually buy expectations of benefits that you promised them, or that they think you promised them," you can help the client form realistic expectations by communicating the nature of the service to be performed, what he may experience, and the outcome to be achieved. In attempting to control customer or client expectations, Cottle (1990, pp. 187-188) also recommends: (1) Avoid the promotional temptation to overpromise. (2) Learn to spot extremist clients in advance, those who think you are messianic or those who think you are just another professional incompetent. (3) Don't oversell the service outcome. (4) Scale down the client's expectations. (5) Introduce the client to the idea of multiple factors outside your control, (6) Educate the client, family and significant others. (7) Stay in touch with the client throughout the service process. This approach reinforces the communicational process that involves techniques of persuasion and teaching through word-of-mouth and mass media channels. Whether or not a company manages and controls public expectations through information and advertising is not our real concern, but whether or not such techniques are employed and how effective they may be in influencing a customer's perception of satisfaction needs to be determined for each situation. There is insufficient data available to endorse all of the above recommendations for managing expectations, but none of them can be discounted or discarded since each may play a role. The same position should be taken regarding the following positions that offer advice on expectation management strategies. Use them retrospectively as points of inquiry, not as cardinal rules.

> **S**uccessful companies manage customer expectations by controlling their advertising and communications.

Beside the communication perspective, two other positions were examined that merit consideration. First, Davidow and Uttal (1989, pp. 83-84) suggest a strategy for managing service. They suggest segmenting customers on the basis of their expectations, finding out what your most important customers expect, and then developing a plan for meeting customer expectations by allowing more delivery time than is actually needed, thereby building in a margin of safety. The approach emphasizes what is important to a core of significant customers and orients services in that direction. But the service provider cannot afford to be one-dimensional. "Services must not only plan for, and adequately perform their core services, but also plan for, and deliver peripheral performance because this is where marketers are truly given the opportunity to go beyond expectations to satisfy customers" (Walker, 1995, p. 12). The peripheral services supporting the main activity can embellish and add the unexpected "treat" that the customer did not anticipate. Second, Barsky (1995, pp. 22-23) sees short- and long-term expectations being influenced by the presentation of the service, the accompanying advertising, the in-facility signage, image, ambience, status symbols, impressions of employees, and other customers. Basically, the emphasis is placed on what the facilities, services, and personnel project in symbolic meaning. It is essential that companies assist customers by making a service tangible (called tangibilizing) through promotional material, and by highlighting the facilities and employees' appearance. Companies also need to implement internal marketing practices that promote effective training and motivation of customer-contact employees. In the extreme, there are always two sides to a perception, so it is best to try strategies that emphasize positive and not negative properties. Left alone without intervention, facilities may project an impression of being warm and inviting or appear stark and cold; some may seem upscale in status or quite dismal in appearance, while employees may project a caring and competent manner or seem inattentive and unprofessional. Such perceptions result in subjective impressions that attach either positive or negative connotations to a place and people, thereby forming expectations.

Perceptions take place continually at different times in the consumption process influencing the content of expectations. But "expectations formed prior to any consumption activity should be qualified. Since these expectations are to a large extent the result of the interactions taking place between the consumer and his/her environment, we can hypothesize that the process of confirmation or disconfirmation of these expectations will be different depending on the nature of the environment as perceived and experienced by the consumer" (Vezina and Nicosia, 1990, p. 39). How the environment is organized, whether it offers many choices or a few, and the availability of information, are among some of the factors affecting expectation formation in a preconsumptive state. Depending upon the tourist provider's failure to succeed in influencing the customer, the overall resulting feelings of satisfaction with a trip are already well established at this stage of the experience. Other perceptions relate more to tangible organizational functions that affect expectations during the trip. These include the consistency in the delivery and quality of the service, innovation in managing change, promotions and marketing efforts, and price. Valuations represent a more concrete set of program attributes that are offered to the customer. While expectations are affected by such program attributes, they are not always apparent, but represent efforts to attract and hold customers. Whether they are effective is measured by how the customer responds, and ultimately, if their expectations are altered by such programs. Expectations are subject to modifications and shifts in direction, and are dynamic throughout a total experience.

Expectations of a customer do not stagnate; they resist change, habituate, or change. Hanan and Karp (1989, p. 2) find that "once satisfied, customers anticipate further satisfaction," while Davidow and Uttal (1989, pp. 12-13) claim that "service expectations are higher today, and will continue growing, because customers are becoming more sophisticated." They argue that expectations rise, placing greater pressure on a company to provide adequate service. However, there is a counter argument that also holds merit; Schneider and Bowen (1995, pp. 24-25) hold that "customers frequently habituate (get used to) certain levels of service such that they are unaware of their expectations regarding the service." The more reliable service delivery is, the more likely customers are to habituate. Violations of habituated expectations can provoke dramatic customer reactions. The acuteness of these situations when they occur can offer an opportunity to learn more about a client's level of expectations and perhaps provide an opportunity to probe other service areas to discover if there are other latent habituated expectations. Whatever the cause, rising expectations or habituated ones, the tourist provider should be prepared "to meet and exceed" expectations (Barsky, 1995, p. 27) in order to preserve and protect the standards established. The result is a constant monitoring process of customer expectations to adjust practice to deal with changes affecting service attributes. To stay on top of changes and meet customer needs, it is often necessary, if not an absolute requirement, to look beyond the confines of your own business situation and examine how others are performing in a similar competitive market niche.

A highly regarded technique for monitoring expectations is called benchmarking, a practice used to measure how successful a competitor actually fulfils customer expectations. Benchmarking is an invaluable tool of self-criticism to answer how much better, worse, or the same your services appear in comparison to your competition, what lessons you can learn from it and how to apply them in your situation, and where competitors just might be better than you in offering a service (Hill, 1992, pp. 50-53). Since expectations are subjective norms and standards that customers create to anticipate a service, it takes non-subjective practices that are provided in a service to verify the intent of an expectation. By using a like competitor as a comparison, the benchmarking company has a way of relatively measuring how well or ill they are doing in fulfilling like expectations with their service practices. In its simplest form, benchmarking is an industry practice of gathering information about your competition through trade journals and other legitimate sources of non-proprietary information or through a formal arrangement to share certain select types of service data with a friendly competitor exclusive and totally divorced from price considerations (Barsky, 1995, Ch. 3-4). It is not just a practice confined to a like competitor, but can be applied to a larger industry segment to measure satisfaction through the fulfillment of expectations. In that respect, Fornell, Johnson, Anderson, Cha, and Byrant (1996) have proposed the American Customer Satisfaction Index (ACSI) that was developed to benchmark various economic sectors and to monitor customer satisfaction from a general U.S. societal perspective. The indicators are few in number: 17 structured questions and eight demographic questions. To date, the index has fallen from the baseline level of 74.5 in 1994 to a low of 73.0 in the first quarter of 1996. In terms of economic sectors, the researchers find satisfaction to be greater for goods than services, and least for the governmental sector. "The decline is driven primarily by the decreasing customer satisfaction with services. To the extent that long-term profitability depends on customer loyalty and the efficiencies gained from long-term buyer-seller relationships, this drop in satisfaction with services should be seen as a warning signal about the long term financial prospects for the firms affected." Since services industries are a large part of the economy, such a decline as a consequence could damage living standards by driving them down. Other studies also confirm the lower ratings for the service sector. Fornell et al. (1996, p. 12) report on comparative studies done by their research team that show "satisfaction higher for goods than for services or retail" in the U.S. In contrast to other national indexes such as Sweden's or Germany's equivalents of the ACSI, a similar pattern is noted. Scores are higher for goods than services, while government or public administration trails behind these other sectors.

The core of the ACSI model contains three concepts viewed as essential variables affecting overall satisfaction. The first is perceived quality or performance, which is the market's evaluation of recent consumption experience. Two key concepts are drawn from the "quality literature" on consumption experience: (a) the degree to which a heterogeneous need is customized to meet the client's needs and (b) the reliability or degree to which a service or product is free of defects and operates in the advertised fashion. The second pertains to the perceived value or the quality of the product or service as measured by the post-purchase experience, relative to the price paid for a given level of value or quality. The third defines the served market's expectations. Customers are asked to recall their knowledge and experiences about the quality of a service or product. Expectations regarding customization, reliability, and overall satisfaction are also measured indicating whether the expectations exceed or fall short of a customer's rating. The ACSI index can be used as a preliminary way of benchmarking a company's overall standing in customer satisfaction. For example, Southwest Airlines has an ACSI score of 76, while the rest of the industry scores on average 69. But benchmarking should be done by determining how a company is positioned in their market relative to the degree of competition they face. Southwest Airlines has certainly exploited their hold on certain routes because of where they fly, but also by deliberately keeping their customers' expectations modest if not low. Determining what factors influence an ASCI score of a company in a business sector relative to their competition opens up avenues of greater understanding about what affects satisfaction and the fulfillment of expectations. Customers not only possess expectations but they also form and possess values and preferences for the kind of tourist service they receive. Those values and preferences are an integral part of the subjective reality of the satisfaction process.

Understanding Values and Preferences

People are generally judgmental about the world around them. In the modern empirical work that probed into the measurement of meaning, the researchers discovered that a majority of human judgments resulted in evaluational conclusions or connotations. A measurement technique, the semantic differential, was developed to study connotative meanings and repeatedly found an evaluational theme in different research situations and among different groups of people

> **Segment tourists by the value they accord to service elements.**

(Osgood, Suci, and Tannenbaum, 1957). Activities and things were judged as being good or bad, favorable or unfavorable, and accorded a value in these terms.

Judgments about a service result in an evaluational position falling along a subjective continuum from highly valued to worthless at the negative extreme. The greater the number of possibilities, the more comparisons of value are made through the decision-making process. "Value is acknowledged or perceived by the customer. Value is also relative, so that competition is indeed a factor in the customer's assessment of value" (De Rose, 1994, p. 18) A judgment of value is made by the customers as they see it, and based upon their individual abilities and experience. There are no absolutes in this process and every judgment has equal weight. The perception of value is so important that Hanan and Karp (1989, p. XII) define a satisfied customer as "one who receives significant added value from a supplier, not simply added product, services, or systems." A service is perceived as being of value only when "satisfaction is the value that has been added to the bottom line of the customer." Hanan and Karp (1989, p. 157) steadfastly believe that "customers are loyal solely and exclusively to value." And loyalty is defined as the "customer's commitment to optimize value." Loyalty to the "greatest satisfaction is the only safe customer guideline a business can follow." The level of satisfaction that a customer associates with a company on judging the value of a service is the standard that a company must be willing to accept or change what they are doing to increase a customers' level of satisfaction.

A key factor that is always part of a customer's perception is pricing and cost as defined in value theory. "Value analysis goes back to the 1940s where a service or product is defined to achieve value at the lowest possible cost of acquisition and use" (De Rose, 1994, p. 12). Simply reducing the price of a service does not automatically increase value. Unfortunately, such a simplistic approach is not an answer but if taken as a "quick fix" usually ends up costing the company even more value in lost sales and lower returns on investment. "Total value is related to perceived costs" (Lele and Sheth, 1991, p. 109). The lower the perceived costs, the higher the value to the customer. An airline ticket, for example, may have a higher monetary cost, but associated costs regarding the availability of time schedules, available days, number of intermediate stops, seating preference, and other customer consideration may be more valuable. Price is only one factor in the analysis of cost.

There are various pricing tactics used to gain insight into the true customer value of a service. For one, "Value pricing . . . quantifies value as it is acknowledged or perceived by the customer" (De Rose, 1994, p. 56). It is common practice to ask customers what kind of price they would put on a service they value, and then provide the estimated company cost, and ask them again to compare both estimates and establish a price level beyond which the service becomes overvalued. Such baseline information assists in establishing regular prices but also helps in offering so-called sale prices. Travel-related companies often hold out special rates and discount fares as do airlines, rental cars, and hotels. These off-peak rates are adjusted to meet the tourist demand in off-business hours and outside of peak demand. Special fares with restrictions are becoming a staple of the airline industry, and customers are playing the fare game. For discretionary travel, such pricing options have become a tactic for increasing value at a lower price. But care must be taken by airlines when advertising destination fares with time limits. One U.S. airline recently offered a reduced fare between Boston and Atlanta that had to begin after 7 p.m., which was possible connecting through Chicago. However, the return starting before 6 a.m. was impossible given their flight schedule out of Boston. That fare was perceived as a bogus value, and reflected poorly on the credibility of the company.

Another tactic to increase a price's value is providing a guarantee (De Rose, 1994, p. 157). A tourist's apprehension about a new experience may be lessened by adding assurance about promises made regarding a choice of destination. But there is the risk of trying to assure a satisfactory result when that service is a result of personal perceptions and expectations. Such guarantees are often viewed with skepticism if stated in vague and too general terms. And given the common practice of overbooking and the canceling of scheduled flights, few in the travel and tourism industry may be willing to provide adequate compensation for delays and shoddy service. Price and guarantees certainly add value but within narrow limits. In the end, however, it is essential that customers are segmented "by the value they place on service, and the kinds of service they expect says a lot about how much service should cost" (Davidow and Uttal, 1989, p. 65). Identifying customers on the basis of value ratings for a service helps set priorities for maintaining and increasing cost efficiency and deciding where personnel emphasis needs to be placed. Hinton and Schaeffer (1994, pp. 39-44) caution that "if you don't ask the right questions of the right people in the right way, you are wasting your money. Your questionnaire should be based on what your customers think is important in doing business with you." The measurement techniques, whether questionnaires, interview schedules, rating forms, panel or focus groups, should reflect the value interests of the customer. Developing those instruments and revamping them is an ongoing process to capture any changes in customer preferences. The emphasis is on what the external customer thinks. But the internal customer, the employee, should also have a role in dealing with the content and specifics of how a service is to be defined and offered since he is ultimately responsible for implementing in-service policies. In conclusion, "customers don't buy services or products. They buy satisfaction of wants. They buy value" (Cannie and Caplin, 1991, p. 59). Delivering an effective service depends on how well value preferences have been ranked to maximize the most value for the least economic and personal costs.

Value Strategies

Business strategies for increasing the value of a service are said to enhance customer satisfaction. These insights are useful as research cues to specific situations but are in no way a substitute for specific customer research. These recommendations to improve and enhance customer satisfaction are synthesized from a variety of situations and may not necessarily apply to everyone. They are more of a guideline than a universal tenet; however, they may offer possible courses of action for the tourist provider. Three strategies, for example, are emphasized by Day (1993, p. 25), beginning with maintaining and increasing value through cost control and pricing of a service. Keeping costs in check from the perspective of the customer is one basic area that should be monitored in a marketing survey to determine whether the customer is receiving good value. Another strategy suggests developing the ability to "tailor services to increasingly fine customer definitions." The real challenge depends on finding creative ways to render a service in a mass market but also tailor it to personal expectations and client values. Finally, keeping in front of changes by exploring innovative ways of introducing new services diffuses much of the turmoil associated with unanticipated change. Fair pricing, personalizing services, and innovations are three strategies that may increase value in a particular situation, but each must be tested for that specific market.

The value of the person as a client is emphasized by Cannie and Caplin (1991, p. 143). They synthesized values centering on the importance of the person and indicated several areas of potential opportunity for improving perceptions of satisfaction. These personal values are worth listing and considering when viewed in actual practice within the tourist industry. Customers "want" dignity and respect, the services to meet their expectations, to feel successful in their travel decision. They also "want" help with problems, to be treated as unique individuals, to be respectful of their limited time, to have someone away from home on their side, to receive benefit from their travel choice, and service providers to treat them as mature adults functioning in multiple roles as family members, professionals, or business people. The values of a person can also be important for enhancing service value. Social values are commonly held beliefs that are shared by particular social groups and found among market segments. A customer's values may be vastly more important to fulfil than pecuniary interests. Reinforcing and appealing to the social beliefs of a customer may significantly increase the value of an experience. Schneider and Bowen (1995, pp. 56-81) believe that a customer's unfulfilled expectations may be violated a number of times without serious consequences just so long as the customer is still receiving "a quality of service superior to the competition." But violate customers' needs or values and they disappointedly abandon the service. The need for "security, esteem, and justice" is seen as being basic to the satisfaction process. The social value model is very adaptable to empirically delineating customer segments. Value-associated interests such as "security, self-respect, and being well respected" are reported by Herche (1994, pp. 11-25). These are most adaptable to consumer relationships. Other value beliefs such as "excitement" and "fun" are the most compatible with tourist interests and are basic leisure stimuli. The value approach, unlike a need theory, has a more parsimonious quality to recommend it and has been successfully used as a survey tool. Such scales might also be associated with how a tourist-customer values a specific service quality attribute. Because travel and tourism is a host industry catering to the world, no group of professionals faces more of a challenge in trying to be true to the above personal tenets. The above list of value strategies notes the importance of providing positive, personal reinforcement for the customer. For a fun-filled industry, the responsibilities in the tourist field are deceivingly complicated and require empathic and caring organizations to provide positive reinforcement.

In weighing an organizational response to a tourist customer, Naumann (1995, p. 20) lists five value lessons stressing the importance of commitment by the organization.

(1) The customer defines the appropriate service quality and price offered. The organization works with the customer through their marketing inquiries in setting service standards and pricing limits.

(2) The customer's expectations are formed relative to competitor alternatives. In a global marketplace, consumers are becoming comparative shoppers by evaluating multiple options to determine the best value at the time. Even shopping the same company for sale opportunities is becoming more prevalent given the posting of fares and rates on the World Wide Web.

(3) The customer's expectations are dynamically changing in response to the rate of competitive activity. New technologies are continually changing the workplace, reducing time spent on minimal repetitive activity not directly servicing the customer. The benefits of labor-saving technologies filter down to the customer, giving companies greater flexibility to try new services, and customers greater opportunities to shift their needs due to new information and innovations.

(4) Service quality is delivered by the total network of people or companies involved in a customer's service selection. It is especially prevalent in the tourism industry that multiple companies and communities are often involved in providing a service. Scheduling, planning, and coordination require unwavering organizational commitment. The tourist operator, travel agent, or destination resort provider collectively share in providing the best possible service, and as a consequence, must blur individual organizational lines and coordinate collectively as if they were a single organization.

> **The lower the perceived costs, the higher the value to the customer.**

(5) Customer value is maximized by the involvement and commitment of the whole organization from top down. A good example is the turnaround of SAS Airlines, whose CEO helped create an extroverted organization relying on the customer as "a moment of truth." Every time a passenger came in contact with an SAS employee who needed to deliver a service, fulfil a request, or answer an inquiry, that was another moment of truth to do it right or fail. In this case, management took the lead in setting a goal to achieve. It seems that successful companies in the service sector possess top management that leave the corporate boardroom and interact with the customer and their own employees on the front line. That kind of leadership inspires employees to do better, and customers are assured that management really cares about their needs.

In summary, value strategies that first reward the customers and place them as a top priority in the line of corporate objectives are typically recognized by the customer as a superior service provider. Offering quality and price to the customer also increases value. Making the organization totally responsible for providing service and operating on that basic premise increases value as companies like Disney, Marriott, SAS, and the Ritz Carlton have discovered. Taking the lead, anticipating change, being innovative, and responding to customer's expectations sets a company apart and potentially increases the perception of value. It must be remembered that the above strategies have to be defined in a specific context and evaluated within that framework to have any merit.

ACHIEVING SATISFACTION

What are some of the philosophies of successful companies for achieving satisfied customers? The Disney Corporation espouses that "high emotional satisfaction and service that exceeds expectations" are what drive clients back to attractions. At an Emory University seminar, given by an instructor from Disney University, it was pointed out that the service goal of the Disney Corporation is to create "happiness" by providing the "finest in entertainment for all ages" (Service, 1997, p. 4). Employees are taught to emphasize four priorities in dealing with the customer, including entertainment, safety, courtesy, and efficiency. The Disney Corporation has made a business out of self-perception over objective reality. "Facts are negotiable but perceptions are not." Since the setting creates the mood and impression at theme parks, attention to detail lies behind much of what the public perceives. The scale may be different for tourism but the reality is much the same— perceptions and positive reinforcement make the difference between a rewarding experience as opposed to a costly waste of discretionary time. The loss for a tourist is not only money and vacation time, but also attitudinal and emotional distress if an experience is unsatisfactory. When that happens, the tourist provider might well wish they had a magic wand to correct the situation. Not everyone will be satisfied

> **K**now what motivates satisfaction "in" and "for" your customer.

in a real world, unlike a magic kingdom, but hopefully that dissatisfied client is not part of a core market. You do not have to satisfy everyone. The Pareto Principle predicts "that 20 percent or fewer of all your customers account for 80 percent or more of your profitable sales volume" (Hanan and Karp, 1989, p. 2). You must achieve dominant customer satisfaction with your core market. It will help you expand and extend your service. It will also guarantee your survival in a competitive market. Yet markets shift, and despite core clients being the heart of corporate profits, the peripheral market may also be a very significant part of operating revenue. Many airlines, hotels, and restaurants, although not specifically developed as a tourist business, use special tourist rates to fill excess capacity in off-core times. Delta Airlines has a core of business travelers but by emphasizing customer satisfaction and service for all passengers is able to attract the pleasure tourist.

But Delta's reputation has suffered this past decade as it has been through a costly expansion, first-time employee layoffs, and a financial slump. But with profits back, Delta is making strides to regain its "image and service" ranking (Thurston, 1997, p. D2). They find themselves muddled in the middle of the pack for on-time service and customer rankings. To change that image, they are taking a number of steps to regain that premier rating. Six years ago, Lele and Sheth (1991, p. 34) reported that "Delta airlines realized that punctuality and timely baggage delivery were crucial to customer satisfaction" and also recognized that superior employee relations are needed to achieve that goal. Delta recently instituted a luggage carry-on program to make it easier for passengers to enter and egress airplanes at the gate. Baggage sizers were installed to quickly determine whether a carry-on bag would fit in the passenger compartment of the aircraft. In the past, customer service was more employee attitude than formal service practice. Today's research, however, still shows that the employee plays a big role in promoting customer satisfaction. The airline has therefore instituted an in-service seminar to re-instill the value of customer service and courtesy to provide service from the heart. The airline has also formed a new review board that meets each month to examine attributes of the service program.

Other successful companies also stress employee service. In the Marriott system, one of the most outstanding resorts is driven by a universal attitude of ensuring guest satisfaction from top management to staff. This is symbolized by the response to a guest: "yes, tell me what you'd like me to do." (Cannie and Caplin, 1991, p. 119). Top management felt that it was easier and more fun to run a hotel filled with happy rather than complaining guests. In the hotel industry, personnel appear to be a major key to winning successful customers. The Hyatt Hotel Corporation also employs a strategy that communicates with the employees, empowers them to act, and to deal with the necessary regulatory requirements. Guest Quarters sees a 50-50 relationship with their employees by providing fair treatment and good benefits in return for customer commitment (Barsky, 1995, pp. 97-104). Besides employee training, more formal guidelines have been proposed to help insure customer satisfaction.

In evaluating guidelines that facilitate satisfaction, Cannie and Caplin (1991) believe that the most successful organizations implement 12 steps to achieve "100 percent customer satisfaction." Successful companies take an organizational top-down management perspective and emphasize a proactive management response beginning with top management commitment. They stress internal evaluation, focus on determining customer requirements, champion the rights of customers, establish customer-performance measures and goals, communicate, motivate, train, and empower employees to solve and prevent problems, and utilize an employee reward and recognition system, followed by continuous improvement. Organizational worksheets and flow charts help sensitize the novice employee. But, there is a hidden danger of becoming so involved with the organization that the customer is lost in the formal guidelines. Organizational guidelines must be compared against the perspective that begins with a client or customer-oriented approach. The goal is not just to deliver a service but how that is accomplished by the employee very often defines a customer's impressions. A balanced approach recognizes the importance of a more customer-oriented perspective by recognizing the central role personnel play in the process.

Another set of guidelines proposed by Naumann (1995, pp. 140-149) outlines 10 basic rules of customer satisfaction that a company should follow. The rules are offered in a condensed version:

(1) Involve top management, not just middle- or lower-level managers with customer satisfaction. Some would say that this is a Japanese approach where top management put themselves at the disposal of middle management and lower level workers.

(2) Know your internal and external customers and what is important to them.

(3) Let your customers define what attributes are important to them regarding what you can deliver.

(4) Know the customers' necessary requirements, what they realistically expect, and what they would want but don't actually expect.

(5) Know the relative importance of the separate attributes of the total service experience.

(6) Gather valid and reliable customer data.

(7) Benchmark yourself against a comparable competitor.

(8) Put plans into action based on data to better implement customer satisfaction.

(9) Continually assess customers and make the results known company-wide to empower all divisions of labor.

(10) Commit to ever improving "our" service that the whole organization takes part in making. This strategy is balanced between the internal and external customer realizing that there needs to be a working relationship for satisfac-

tion to blossom. This approach also balances customer data gathering and benchmarking data against competition. It also balances reliable data gathering against continually engaging in customer data assessment that is shared with employees. And finally, it recognizes that all levels of the organization's management and workers are mutually involved in providing service.

To summarize, most of the experts believe that it takes both the customer and employee to achieve a measure of satisfaction. Personnel play an important role, and customer evaluational data are the real report card against which satisfaction is measured.

CONCLUSION

The evolution of the customer-satisfaction concept is still being refined. The genesis of how it is defined and measured has progressed by building upon a model that was already well established by the late 1970s. The model is simply built upon the central premise and assumption that the customer decides what is important and valuable for achieving personal satisfaction. In determining customer satisfaction, three key concepts operationalize how a measure of satisfaction is calculated. "Expectations provide the foundation for customers to compare their experiences" (Barsky, 1995, p. 39). Identifying gaps between customer preferences and expectations, what they expect, and what kind of quality (value) they receive determines satisfaction. It is necessary to measure what a customer expects, values, and prefers to obtain a reliable and valid reading of customer satisfaction in any tourist situation.

In order to achieve a goal of providing satisfaction, a number of strategies are reviewed to determine what the experts in the field have determined positively or negatively affects the customer's perceptions. Foremost, understanding what the customer expects is basic, and then establishing a fixed level of service that can be reliably delivered is fundamental. Being receptive and open to customers' input is also another very basic practice for increasing satisfaction. Expectations are not passive norms but change with the customer. Expectations are managed and techniques such as the following are outlined for companies to employ: Segment customers use advertising and pricing promotions, and actively manage the ambience of the situation.

Values and preferences are another essential element in understanding and affecting customer satisfaction. Pricing alone is simply not the only value a company controls. Being innovative with a service, being cognizant of time constraints, and personalizing a service add value to an experience. Most important, treating the customer with respect and courtesy increases the value of an experience. As a result, customer satisfaction is increased through value-added service.

Customer satisfaction is a consequence of perceived value, expectations, and positive reinforcement. It results from the deliberate, proactive actions taken by a company. This inquiry also contains an overview of various guidelines that successful companies have adopted to increase and enhance satisfaction. These guidelines are the product of business research and expert experience. They merit consideration because of the insightful cues offered into how a customer's perceptions may be influenced.

If understanding of a customer's response is a goal, and if a satisfactory response of a customer plays such a significant role in the success of an enterprise, then it is crucial that the tourist provider understand how to maximize satisfaction through service. Just as tourism and satisfaction are linked, so too is providing service and satisfaction, which will be explored in the next chapter.

The performance of the tourist providers at each stage in the process is important for establishing the right conditions for a satisfying experience.

■ 2

Service Quality and Satisfaction

WHY SATISFACTION AND CUSTOMER SERVICE?

Conditional Influences on Service Satisfaction

THE COHESIVENESS that binds together a pleasure trip and makes it either an exciting positive or disappointing negative experience rests to some extent on the quality of the service rendered. The performance of the tourist providers at each stage in the process is important for establishing the right conditions for a satisfying experience. The basic and essential services of providing information, food, transportation, shelter, and a safe, secure environment establish the necessary basic foundation upon which a vacation or holiday is organized. Without an efficiently coordinated infra-service structure to facilitate some of these necessities, the effort and risk for a tourist is far too costly in time and a personal-involvement burden. Life in a modern global village already contains its share of struggles without adding another burden, especially when a consumer is looking forward to a rewarding and relaxing tourist experience.

It is not just the mechanics of a trip involving the planning, preparation, and packing that raise social costs, but also the emotional involvement that is not yet fully understood. Satisfaction is not purely a rational process. Customer satisfaction "may be more than a simple cognitive evaluative process. Rather it is probably a complex human process involving extensive cognitive, affective and other undiscovered psychological and physiological dynamics" (Oh and Parks, 1997, p. 37). Taking this broader theoretical perspective opens up a greater range of possibilities for understanding what affects customer service. While customer-service providers directly create either negative or positive conditions, the tourist experience is also influenced by the nature of the activity, the customer's emotional involvement, the exchange process, and the consumer institutions. Both the emotional nature of an activity and the broader consumer institutions are reinforcing factors that shape a tourist response toward satisfaction or dissatisfaction. These factors are intertwined in the service situation, and they are not so likely to be easily manipulated in a specific tourist context.

Since tourism is a manifestation of leisure activity, a hedonic emotional feeling influences satisfaction. But tourists are not just conditioned to a simplistic, emotional situation where only pleasurable feelings are anticipated. Tourists are capable of multiple emotional responses that influence satisfaction responses. In defining emotional effects on satisfaction, Krishnan and Olshavsky (1995, p. 454) describe and test "a dual role" where emotions are separately analyzed within the context of the actual consumption process and in sharp contrast during the post or evaluation phrase. This dual role of emotions may be especially important when "hedonistic attributes" are involved in the satisfaction process. "For instance, consumers may be extremely frightened (a negative emotion) about a roller coaster ride, but their evaluation of this experience may be joyful (a positive emotion) since they wanted to be frightened. These direct affective experiences may provide particularly strong influences on overall satisfaction for products/services that are primarily hedonic in nature." Even in the pre-consumptive process, consumers in approaching hedonic situations often describe their expectations in "terms of specific emotions" as well as in terms of the intensity of an emotion. For example, a trip may be both very exciting and also relaxing. Preliminary findings from the above exploratory research provide initial support for a dual model. This finding "alerts researchers to the possibility that the emotion experienced during consumption is conceptually different from evaluations of this emotion." Krishnan and Olshavsky (1995, p. 459) advise that "future studies should have separate measures of those emotions that result directly from hedonic experience and those that result from a comparison process." Clear-cut emotional descriptions and degrees of affectation are likely to be quite complex in real situations where emotional reactions may contain mixed responses. Ryan (1995, p. 60) describes such a situation where feeling and satisfaction diverge. "In the short term the queasy stomach, the mosquito bite, and other such holiday experiences can produce unpleasant feelings of a distinct lack of well-being, yet the holiday experience can still be judged satisfactory. The important point, however, is that a general sense of well-being and perception of life being 'satisfactory' can be derived from a holiday, even when events within that holiday might be less than ideal." Emotional research potentially adds another behavioral explanation to the satisfaction process that affects how salient an attribute is ranked by a customer. In tourist situations, some attributes such as weather, insects, and queasy stomachs are not under direct management control but may trigger strong emotional responses. Future studies into tourist satisfaction are likely to explore more fully the role of emotions in the actual and post-evaluative context and what triggers such responses.

In addition to the emotional conditions influencing the consumer, the attributes of the exchange process within society also influence satisfaction. Vezina and Nicosia (1990, pp. 37, 39) ascribe the status of a social institution to the consumption process in which a series of norms develop to handle transactions by enforcement through the "mechanisms of rewards and sanctions." Satisfied customers are successful at purchasing tourist services and acquiring value and quality at a fair price. Tourist merchants and consumers are part of a dynamic social exchange process. Exchange norms are not static denominators in a society and are subject to change. As a consequence, not all consumers will equally adapt to changes. There are always innovators and early adapters along with those consumers who remain laggards and change resistors. Consumers who adapt to change most likely tend to possess a higher socioeconomic status, are more cosmopolitan in outlook, and are themselves considered to be opinion leaders in the community. These "consumers will adopt and conform more easily and rapidly to the norms enforced by the consumption institutions, and hence experience a greater level of satisfaction out of their consumption activities." Because the role of the consumer dominates such a large part of our lives, Vezina and Nicosia (1990, pp. 36-37) claim that "consumption is an important activity in everybody's life." It is even taking an increasing importance with respect to almost any possible criterion because it is related to "overall life satisfaction." This perspective is based upon becoming a skilled consumer that translates into how satisfactorily the consumer actually manages and negotiates the pre- and post-purchasing process.

In retrospect, two conditional factors are seen as intervening influences on the customer-service process: emotional responses and the level of consumer skills are essentially psychological and learned responses that affect levels of satisfaction experienced within the service process. Hedonistic emotional possibilities increase within a tourist situation to ensure value while consumer skills are vital in the planning and purchasing process.

Customer Service and Satisfaction

Most people living in the United States in the early 1800s made a living by fishing, hunting, growing crops, or raising cattle. Later, America stood as an industrial giant manufacturing most everything out of its shops and foundries. America has now become a post-industrial society, where many of today's employed work in the service sector. In a recent review, Walker (1995, p. 5) refer-

> **Tourists are capable of multiple emotional responses that influence satisfaction responses.**

ences a number of sources to show that in comparison to the general economy, services have grown until they currently account for over two-thirds of America's GNP, employing three-quarters of the American workforce, and are being counted on to help offset the balance of trade. Sun and Uysal (1994, p. 71) found that Disney theme parks are attracting more tourists and visitors than the leading international tourist destinations. If the hotel, transportation, and supporting theme destinations, both commercial and public, are factored into the equation, a sizable benefit is generated by the tourism-hospitality service sector. The tourist industry is big business for America.

Types of service should also be evaluated with respect to the importance of the benefit to the consumer (Vezina and Nicosia, 1990, p. 40). The key to service satisfaction is based upon how important and significant that activity is viewed through the perceptions and expectations of the consumer. The bottom line is the direct benefit to the consumers and what they value as a beneficial travel experience.

Equating customer service with offering value means also including the value of personal satisfaction. "Customer service means all features, acts, and information that suggest the customer's ability to realize the potential value of a core product or service" (Davidow and Uttal, 1989, p. 22). Such a definition concentrates on the value of how the services are used and what is expected by the customer. If a tourist enterprise offers multiple services and some are not used, then no one benefits. It is simply a matter of survival in the competitive world that service personnel at all levels of the organization remain alert to customer shifts in preference, so that service changes can be initiated.

Customer service is a set of activities that is premised on client satisfaction that adds value due in part to the continued process of improving a service system. According to De Rosa (1994, p. 139) most companies view customer service "as an ancillary activity of other processes rather than a value-contributing process in its own right." If there is no recognition, especially in the tourist sector, that service generates value, then companies who are part of the system are sure to fail. The Bahamas bound tourist discovered some years ago that there are other islands in tropical waters with sea, sun, and surf that are more than willing to provide quality service. A big danger for anyone working as a tourist provider is adhering to a focus solely on destination(s). A broader perspective is needed to view the client and tourist as a customer by sorting out what core technical or functional attributes are most meaningful in a travel experience. Although services are "bundles of attributes rendering satisfaction, services are primarily intangible, cannot be separated from their provider or stored in inventory, and their delivery tends to be inconsistent" according to Walker (1995, pp. 5-6, 11). Service performance is divided into technical and functional, in which the core service of what the customer receives fulfils the technical requirements while the how, where, when, and why deal with the functional or supplemental attributes. To illustrate the differences between the two, "a hotel's core service could be described as a comfortable night's rest" while its functional attributes may include "a room easily accessible from the elevator, a pleasant desk clerk, or room service." Companies frequently concentrate effort on the core service, which often becomes a common commodity in an imitative competitive market. They should be looking at all aspects of service including those functional attributes that may offer a distinctive advantage or edge over their competition. To enhance recognition of excellent service, customers should be provided an appropriate focus by "tangibilizing the service," by using visible symbols such as "placing a mint on the pillow of a freshly made bed or a sanitary covering on a clean glass." Creative ways should be tested to help customers notice aspects of services that promote increased satisfaction.

Walker adopted (1995, p. 7-11) from the earlier work of Fisk (1981) a three-stage evaluation process in an effort to better understand how core technical and functional attributes affect service. A service encounter is separated into distinct pre-consumptive, consumptive, and post-consumptive stages that "help a manager to see both the core and peripheral (functional) component influences of their offerings." For a manager or employee, this helps establish a more clearly defined and distinct outline of service concentration. At stage one, consumers encounter "peripheral components," the introductory phase of the service where evidence about the quality is being formed. The customer seeks out physical and tangible cues to quality simply because they require a minimum of commitment and interaction. If the customer is new to the situation, expectations are likely to be "passive in nature" and not fully formed so it is much easier for them to interact with the surroundings. In visiting the relatively new Boston Harbor Hotel facing the ocean, a number of tangible attributes help form a positive impression. First, the setting or physical location on the water with a view of the harbor, a planted-landscaped walk along the ocean with spacious views from the lobby, and public meeting rooms set a very positive and inviting tone. The visual preference literature repeatedly affirms strong positive support for settings with water (Noe and Hammitt, 1988). Second, the interior stage is comprised of open public corridors and rooms at different levels that flowed into one another presenting the customer with an ease of movement yet a sense of not being overpowered, a kind of understated elegance. Third, the scene and decor for the public entrance and rooms are comprised of rich warm colors, indirect lighting, lush carpeting, and small clusters of upholstered, color-coordinated furniture, wood and floral accent pieces to attract the eye. Fourth, servers dressed in distinctive clothing at the curb, the counters, and in the public areas symbolize a function that is clean, neat, and polished. They are informed, polite, friendly, accommodating, and trained before being put on the front line. "A growing atmospherics literature attests to the importance of managing the physical environment" (Walker, 1995, p. 8). At stage two, the customer enters the core of the service which they are primarily interested in acquiring. Continuing with the Boston Harbor Hotel as an example, a number of activities are simultaneously being organized and orchestrated by the staff during one small part of the day that illustrate how the customer's focus shifts at this stage. Not least among the services offered is providing clean, well-appointed lodging for rest and comfort. But also a wedding rehearsal, catered dinner parties, a wine-tasting seminar, and numerous private small groups and individuals are meeting and being served in the restaurant and lounge. At this stage in the consumptive phase, the customer's focus on the product and the providers in delivering the service at a fair price is essential to the experience. It is at this stage that the professional training, scheduling, personnel needs, and problem-solving abilities of management and staff are tested and where attention to detail does not go unnoticed by the satisfied customer. This represents the best that the staff and management can offer. At stage three, the post-core service begins where again more peripheral functions take over the service that facilitates an easy exit. At the Boston Harbor Hotel, the staff also switches to a more passive role where they are conveniently placed to give directions or answer questions. In this stage, a sense of efficiency and promptness is displayed by staff who move the top coats and belongings of a group attending a seminar and dinner from the original point of entry to the new point of egress, making it more convenient for the customers to collect their belongings. Prepayment arrangements are in place, making it easy for a large group to settle their accounts without long lines or waits. A protocol of etiquette is displayed by the staff that helps pave the way in exiting without a sense of being rushed or hurried. The customers are made to feel relaxed and respected as they make their way to the exits. The staff creates a positive, past-tense impression in the mind of the patrons who loved being there and being pampered. The major factor that increases the value of the service is the manner and training that the staff demonstrated in their interactions with the customer. Certainly, the tangible attributes of the setting also contributed to the enhancement of the service, but collectively it takes the internal customer, the staff, to bring everything together, to make it work for the customer. Organizations that are customer-oriented and who are especially organized in the pre-consumptive and post stages of delivering a service generate more value for themselves and their patrons.

In a review of literature regarding service quality and satisfaction in the hospitality industry, Oh and Parks (1997, pp. 35-38) cite widespread support among management experts and researchers for profitability and increased occupancy rates in customer-oriented organizations. They are of the opinion that "more rigorous theoretical and methodological treatments" are needed to advance an understanding of service quality and satisfaction. Of the research approaches reviewed, they note that the expectancy-disconfirmation model has received the widest acceptance among practitioners since it has been interpreted in other theoretical explanations giving a more expanded perspective to understanding satisfaction. They give credit to Barsky (1992) for integrating "attributes" of lodging and disconfirmation theory, which confirmed that satisfaction was related to the interplay of a customer's perceptions, expectations, and intentions. The goal of any science is to provide a more parsimonious explanation, but if attribute analysis is used solely by the hospitality industry to identify satisfaction, then the list is virtually unlimited. But that is not a problem *per se*; data reduction and clustering techniques can reduce the number of attributes empirically. Disconfirmation theory, however, provides an explanation for differentiating between attributes and transcends a particular situation. In the following section in this chapter, various applications of the service quality and the disconfirmation model are reviewed to offer more detailed insight into how the model is applied in service situations. However, most applications of the SERVQUAL model are found in field surveys that Oh and Parks (1997, pp. 36, 42-43) think should be expanded to experimental or longitudinal (panel) designs. But given their view of the "incipient" status of the research, the question probably needs more time to be re-examined in case studies of a cross-sectional nature without the risk of a long-term study that is premature or experimental designs that have no solid bases for manipulating variables. Despite impatience with the progress of research, Oh and Parks (1997, p. 54) are correct in suggesting the feasibility of integrating service quality (SQ) and consumer satisfaction (CS) in hospitality research. "Even statistically, the inclusion of SQ and CS in the same model seems to work well." Also, both models, when related to customers' "behavioral intentions, appear to enhance the predictability of consumer satisfaction." The same could be said for tourism research as well. To summarize, the quality of service is an attitudinal disposition related to the total service package, while satisfaction is related to a specific attribute transaction. Over time, the cumulative incidents of satisfaction consolidate into an attitude toward the value of a service. The responses of a customer to the attributes of a service form a basis for understanding what may be satisfying or dissatisfying.

CUSTOMER SERVICE GAPS

Gaps in Expectations and Service Delivery

A gap is a space or distance in service between what is expected and actually realized by the customer. Table 1 illustrates the service gap model that is based on an understanding of expectations.

> **Creative ways should be tested to help customers notice aspects of services that promote increased satisfaction.**

In explaining the gap model, Walker (1995, p. 6) holds that researchers generally agree that consumer satisfaction results from a subjective comparison of expected and perceived attribute levels. These cognitive affective comparisons produce evaluations that lead to negative disconfirmation/dissatisfaction, confirmation/neutrality, or positive confirmation/satisfaction. Unless something unexpected occurs prior to, during, or after purchase, a customer's evaluation of his service encounter will include increasing amounts of neutral judgments. However, if the unexpected occurs, then the service performance is judged as being below or above one's expectation and leads to satisfaction or dissatisfaction. Judging the quality of the service process begins with understanding the nature of the expected. Just as attributes of a service change for different kinds of service, expectations are subject to differences. The most fundamental of differences results between a material product and a less tangible service. "Customers have very different expectations about services than they do about products. Further, they have different kinds of expectations for different kinds of services, just as they have different kinds of expectations for different kinds of products" (Schneider and Bowen, 1995, pp. 20-21). For a service organization, expectations are specifically less tangible, meaning that the performance, delivery, and execution take precedent. Very simply, "service yields psychological experiences more than it yields physical possessions. It is acts and processes more than the physical attributes of a product that determine customer satisfaction in a service business" (Schneider and Bowen, 1995, pp. 19-20). Service still takes place within a tangible social situation, but the emphasis is focused on the process that is judged subjectively by the customer. But there are times within that

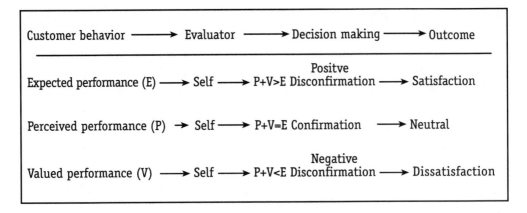

Table 1:
Gap model of customer service satisfaction

subjective process that customers do not possess an expectation and find themselves in a zone of indifference. That state of indifference, however, is a kind of neutral expectation.

Expectations are pivotal to understanding the decision process. According to Fornell et al. (1996, p. 14), customer expectations establish a normative standard for predicting "quality, value, and customer satisfaction." A number of qualifying conditions, however, come into play in assessing where expectations have the greatest impact on decisions. "If a particular good or service is difficult to standardize or quality is unambiguous, variance in consumption experience is greater and expectations should have less influence." Similarly, in areas of consumption where a customer makes frequent and routine purchases, expectations should have greater weight. "When such interactions are less frequent, customers have less direct knowledge and their expectations should be weaker predictors of perceived quality and value. The findings for the direct association between expectations and satisfaction are similar." For many businesses in the tourism destination, where purchases are less frequent, expectations might be weak but where standards of quality are more sharply defined as in transportation and hospitality, expectations are perhaps more significant in determining satisfaction. When price or cost, however, enters into the comparison, satisfaction is highest in the airline transportation sector but less significant in the hospitality service area, where quality and customization apparently mean more to the customer. In those sectors where price plays a greater role in determining satisfaction, company loyalty is lower where switching behavior is based on who has the better deal at that time. Factors affecting satisfaction such as expectations, customization, reliability, and price facilitate customers' perceived evaluation of an experience. Knowledge of how these factors act and interact in the satisfaction process afford valuable insights into how a company might alter their impact on customers' satisfaction by emphasizing one factor over another. Yet, factors such as price and customization of service are superseded by expectations that are formed around these and other factors. In the end, the importance of influencing the formation and setting of expectations is necessary, if not essential, for a tourist enterprise because "When expectations exceed perceived levels of service, customers are pleasantly surprised and highly satisfied" (Davidow and Uttal, 1989, p. 80).

Companies succeeding at providing customer satisfaction "must operate near the top if not above the zone of tolerance" to "create a reputation for superior service" (Berry, Parasuraman, and Zeithaml, 1993, p. 14). This means that a company consistently exceeds the expectation rankings of the customer. But some critics argue that this is impossible because, as noted in the last chapter, expectations change, habituate, or rise. Such fluctuations in expectations are not impossible barriers but offer a continual challenge to monitor service attributes for quality. The dynamism of expectations, though always subject to change, may not be subject to wild swings and trends. "America's service customers want the basics. They expect service companies to do what they are supposed to do; they expect fundamentals, not fanciness, performance, not promises. In all of our customer research, we have yet to find any evidence of extravagant customer expectations." In the case of hotels, customers want "clean, quite, comfortable, secure rooms in good working order" (Berry et al., 1993, pp. 7-8). What is expected today as clean in a hotel room may not be what is anticipated in the future. Technology, materials, practices, and personnel change, all of which may change expectations. Repeat visitors to a hotel or resort may find their stay less than satisfying on repeat stays. Since expectations will change, so "should your ability to meet and exceed them" (Barsky, 1995, p. 27). If expectations are not met or exceeded, a gap is created leading to customer dissatisfaction.

The best application of the service quality model is essentially reserved for identifying breakdowns in service satisfaction according to Naumann (1995) who follows the lead of Parasuraman, Zeithaml, and Berry (1984). Instead of viewing gaps exclusively from the perspective of just the customer, Naumann (1995, pp. 94-98) also emphasizes areas where management fails. For example, if customer expectations are misunderstood by management, a "research" gap exists; if management's service delivery systems are incapable of fulfilling the customers expectations, "a planning and design" gap exists; if the delivery system is incapable of providing customer satisfaction because the internal customer, the employee, fails to respond, an "implementation" gap exists; if the delivery system is not described properly for the customer, a "communication" gap exists; and finally, if the customer's perceptions and expectations do not match, a "reality" gap exists. A reality gap is unlikely to occur, however, if the other four gaps are closed in the organization. For the most part, the gap model is viewed from the vantage point of the customer, but Naumann integrates the employee's perspective that should not be overlooked in the SERVQUAL gap model. Hopefully, the following analysis will provide a more balanced view since the interactions of the customer and employee are partners in the service act.

A Service Quality Gap Model

The SERVQUAL model defines a gap between what the customer perceives and expects. The core of the model is the range of expectations a customer may possess, labeled "the zone of tolerance." This represents the limits of customer satisfaction bounded at one end by a "desired level and at the other end by adequate service levels" (Parasuraman, Zeithaml, and Berry, 1994, Summary, pp. 1-2). This particular installment of the SERVQUAL model tests different measurement formats for detecting service adequacy and superiority. Both from a psychometric and diagnostic analysis, this report should be consulted because of its methodological and practical measurement import for obtaining a better understanding. The findings of this report are grounded in empirical research on how to deal with expectancy levels. The authors argue that managers obtain a truer assessment by incorporating the possibility of different ratings of desired and minimum perceived service. Desired service represents a blend of what customers believe "can be" and "should be" provided, while minimum service represents what the customer is willing to accept. The relative difference between the two marks a "zone of tolerance" that may be very narrow for some service quality dimensions and broader for others. By defining expectations within this range of satisfaction, the "diagnostic utility of the measurement increases since each service attribute (reliability, responsiveness, assurance, empathy, tangibles) can be examined separately to determine where shortfalls in service may be occurring as well as determining where the strength of a service is centered." To test perceptions and mark the zone of desired to minimum expectations, Parasuraman et al. (1994, p. 34) examined and tested direct versus difference scoring procedures. "The results indicate that the difference-score measure perform as well as the direct measures on all psychometric criteria except predictive power" or explaining variance. If predictive utility is the major objective then a direct, perceptions-only scale is the best. "However, if identifying critical service shortfalls is the principle objective, then a three-column difference format questionnaire seems most useful." In this case, desired versus minimum levels of expectation are being measured. The customer's perception of a service attribute is also taken into account at the same time. The advantage of a three-format scale allows for a single-attribute, diagnostic evaluation that is most important for improving service by determining where the shortfalls are taking place. It is the recommendation of the above authors that "companies consider adopting a service quality measurement system that produces separate measures of minimum service and desired service expectations and perceptions of service performance. This research format captures both the predictive and diagnostic considerations for understanding more completely the effectiveness of service attributes."

Numerous practitioners and researchers have adopted this model, but not necessarily the above three-pronged research format. In adopting this gap model without the research format, Cottle (1990, p. 268) emphasizes the attributes of service quality by stressing the *reliability* of a service, providing *assurance* that the customer is dealing with capable people, demonstrating *tangible* signs of service through appearance, and by being *responsive* and *empathetic* in showing that you care about your customer relationships. Barsky (1995, pp. 32-33) also recommends the so-called RATER model for ensuring quality service. The (R)eliability-dependability, (A)ssurance, knowledge, and courtesy of staff, the (T)angibles of physical appearance, (E)mpathy toward the customer, and (R)eponsive-prompt service are widely endorsed and accepted in the service sector.

In comparing the importance of attributes across SERVQUAL studies, reliability of service is the most important and rates highest among customer concerns. Responsiveness in providing prompt service is next, followed by the assurance of the employees' ability to convey trust and confidence, and also project an empathetic caring manner. Rated last were the tangible appearance of the physical plant, personnel, equipment, and the approaches used to communicate with the customer. Responsiveness, assurance, empathy, and a tangible appearance are "process dimensions" and most important in "exceeding customer expectations" that are accomplished by surprising the customer with the unexpected, while reliability is an outcome dimension where promises of service need to be kept (Berry et al., 1993, pp. 4-5, 12). Because service situations are not always solely associated with economic functions, differences are likely to arise in other sociological situations. To examine this assertion, Crompton and Mackay (1988) carried out a groundbreaking study on the SERVQUAL model among recreational activities, including a comparison of a travel option. The comparative approach of the researchers in evaluating differences and similarities between recreational activities is used to test the following two hypotheses "that dimensions of service quality will not be of equal importance to participants in selected recreation programs and across selected recreation programs." Comparisons are analyzed between four different types of recreation including painting classes, fitness classes, hockey, and trips. Of the five service quality dimensions, responsiveness and empathy are higher for respondents taking painting classes; assurance is rated higher by trip respondents. Tangibles are higher for the hockey players, and for the fitness group, reliability was the highest rated quality. However, reliability is important for all recreation activities, but especially for a sport such as hockey or fitness where performance is important. Since travel and tourism is of most interest, in addition to assurance being most important, respondents in the trip program are "particularly emphatic about the relative importance of reliability and the relative unimportance of empathy" (Crompton and Mackay, 1988, pp. 371-374). As travel situations are more differentiated in future research, the relative significance of attributes might shift in importance.

In addition to evaluating the above service attributes, Parasuraman et al. (1994, p. 25) also examined service consequences by determining the behavioral intentions of the customers as a result of their experiences with the quality of the service performances. In the study, five categories of behavioral intentions are identified. These deal with actions expressing loyalty to a company, a propensity to switch to a competitor, a willingness to consider price increases or pay more for a service, an internal response to a problem by complaining to employees, and an external response to a problem by complaining to other consumers or outside agencies. The results of the research confirm that loyalty and willingness to pay more are positively correlated with service quality, while a propensity to switch to another company and engaging in external responses to a problem are negatively correlated with service quality. The internal response to a problem of complaining to employees is nonsignificant. The direction of the predicted correlation demonstrates that customer behaviors support and reinforce superior service. If expectations are not met or exceeded, negative responses prevail that are injurious to a company's future.

In conjunction with understanding the SERVQUAL model, a relatively up-to-date service compendium is available and identifies some "lessons" for improving service quality (Berry et al., 1993). The lessons are summarized below because they flow from the theory of expectations. This is an excellent source to learn more about these researchers' work, and much of what they recommend follows from these practices. "Little else matters to customers when the service is unreliable," so the center and key to service is reliability. The remaining lessons function on behalf of the customer when the organization listens to the internal and external customer on improving service. "The service system should be designed to deliver the basic service with excellence." American customers want fundamentals, not frills, so design a service situation with convenience in mind. Design flaws can reduce quality; for example, "hotel rooms with such poor lighting that guests are discouraged from any nighttime activity requiring visual acuity; or computer-generated billing statements that are impossible for customers to understand" are examples pertinent to design gaps (Berry et al., 1993, p. 8). Utilization of test settings or on-site prototypes helps define and refine designs making them more efficient. When practices break down or accidents happen, a recovery plan should clearly outline courses of action. Implementing a recovery service plan usually provides an opportunity to surprise customers and to demonstrate fair play. Customers have to try a service and assess whether it treats them fairly. "It is not a separate dimension of service; it is the very essence of what customers expect." Hotel guests complain when hotels do not honor guaranteed reservations which is considered an unfair action (Berry et al., 1993, p. 14). Being just, impartial, and keeping promises helps assure a company's good reputation. And finally, teamwork, employee research, and servant leadership sensitivity are critical factors in an organization's emotional readiness to deliver quality service. Cannie and Caplin (1991, p. 118) also provide a checklist of customer-oriented service qualities or lessons that include stressing the tangible appearance, reliability, and responsiveness in delivering service. They also recommend developing communication skills and projecting a credible, competent, and courteous demeanor, offering security in transactions, being understanding, and being accessible to the customer. Not surprisingly, the lessons closely parallel those of Berry et al. (1993) and further reinforce the need for such positive, management service practices.

Oh and Parks (1997, p. 49), however, have leveled some criticism of the SERVQUAL model in hospitality research. They report discrepancies in the number of service quality dimensions but offer only untested possibilities for these discrepancies ranging from the (1) structural or organizational differences of service quality across services, (2) situational differences relating to performance and expectations, and (3) differences in "factor abstraction achieved by researchers," presumably in the application of factor or other data-reduction techniques. Perhaps it is also possible that the modifications of the hospitality studies, as reported by Oh and Parks (1997), are themselves the cause of these differences. In any case, their work encourages refinements in the direction of future customer satisfaction (CS) and service quality (SQ) studies and the expansion of certain aspects to improve the value of the SERVQUAL model. Many studies have unduly emphasized only what affects CS and SQ. However, there are different industry concerns, such as "knowing and predicting the consequences of CS and SQ and understanding their link to customers' long-term attitudes and future purchase decision," Oh and Parks (1997, p. 40). Such an emphasis concentrates on the customer's future dispositions or attitudes emerging about various aspects of their service experience or about what previous satisfaction attributes trigger customers' decisions to purchase in the future. Both aspects may be used by management to redesign more positive customer programs.

Understanding service attributes in different types of situations is important to better measure variations in the level of service provided and hopefully develop a parsimonious set of behavior-based, market-specific service attributes. Moreover, other measurement concerns need to be pursued relating to scale improvement, clarifying expectation criteria, matters of reliability and validity, and hypothesis-directed research. Some of these, such as expectations and intentions, are already being addressed (Parasuraman et al., 1994) and should in time make their way into the hospitality and tourism research. Perhaps also in time, extraneous intervening variables will also cross over from more product-oriented to service research. Future research might also begin to apply such distinctions and refinements in specific service situations (Patterson, 1993) as found in the research on involvement by Ladki and Nomani (1996). As the service gap model evolves through application and change, customer satisfaction and service performance in tourism research will more sharply define the role relationships between the customer traveler and tourist provider.

SERVICE PROVIDERS AND RECIPIENTS

Internal Customers

The Japanese introduced the notion of internal and external customers. The internal customer is the corporate producer, while the external customer is the outside consumer of the service. Satisfaction is essential to both parties to make things work. Just as customers have expectations about service delivery, employees too share expectations. Heskett, Sasser, and Schlesinger (1997) find a mutually supporting link to corporate profit between employee satisfaction and customer satisfaction. Just as customers have expectations about service delivery, employees, too, share expectations about how to conduct themselves in providing a service.

Unemployment levels today are near a 24-year low in the U.S. The labor market is tight for both skilled and unskilled employees. Couple low employment with steady growth, and it is even harder to compete for good employees. A tourist or hospitality company is hard pressed to provide a quality service if it cannot retain and satisfy its own employees. According to the American Hotel Motel Association, average turnover at full-service hotels is 100 percent and 300 percent at economy hotels. Because wages are so competitive, hourly employees will leave for as little as 10 cents an hour. Since the late 1930s, the guru of management, Peter Drucker, has been preaching that the most important asset of a company is its employees. In the service section, it is most important to have employees who are happy and like what they are doing for the public. If they are unhappy and dissatisfied, the external employee, the customer, will probably experience a loss in the quality of the service. Service companies such as the Marriott Corporation realize that what they sell is "what they deliver" (Rauscher, 1997b) and in order to retain employees have started employee-assistance programs. A 24-hour hotline that is being field tested in Atlanta is designed to assist employees with personal problems. They are also implementing a 24-hour, subsidized day care, and established an in-house medical office where employees can receive basic medical services during working hours. Marriott estimates that for every dollar spent on employee programs, they can save four dollars through greater productivity and less absenteeism. Other hotels are experimenting with profit-sharing programs and other incentive-based programs. What has happened in other corporations will happen in the hospitality and tourism industry. Successful in-house service programs will eventually become stand-alone subsidiaries offering the service to their competition. In destination resorts with a concentration of hotels and restaurants, more corporations will begin to explore such adjunct business services as a way of retaining experienced employees.

A most important part of any employee service program is listening to what employees have to say about the way services are managed and how improved situations can be made more efficient. Berry et al. (1993, pp. 15-18) find that employee teamwork and listening to frontline employees really function as an early warning system in critically judging and detecting breakdowns in a delivery system that is central to providing an "excellent service." As part of the delivery system, employee-oriented management succeeds when leadership skills are encouraged that foster a kind of "servant leader" who teaches, inspires, coaches, and helps fellow employees. The Sheraton Corporation, for example, conducts an annual employee survey relating to the issue of employee relations, benefits, and communication with management and whether the employees feel that they can satisfy their guests through the organization. In an effort to bring the organization to the employee, the Sheraton has decentralized its operations into separate employee functions that operate from within rather than having a top-down management directive for daily operations. The employees are empowered to make those decisions within their operating units, be it housekeeping, food, or beverage. Other hotel corporations use employee focus groups to regularly determine what employee work concerns are being addressed or not addressed. A chain such as the Ritz-Carlton Hotels employs an Internal Defect Report, where it is the responsibility of each and every employee to report a defect. The management team has 48 hours to investigate, verify, and recommend a course of action (Hinton and Schaeffer, 1994, pp. 72-77). In this approach, information input is brought down to the level of the frontline employee who is empowered to alert the management team of possible service breakdowns. Unlike other passive forms of input that take time to work through a system, this proactive approach is quick and direct, but requires an increased commitment and involvement from every level of employee.

> *The SERVQUAL model defines a gap between what the customer perceives and expects.*

Developing a highly selective hiring process which identifies those individuals most likely to mesh with the company's philosophy facilitates the building of a satisfied work force. Davidow and Uttal (1989, pp. 112-117) cite Embassy Suites hotel for providing a quality service experience with caring, competent, responsive, helpful, and friendly service by targeting the business travelers who make up two-thirds of their clients, and those families with children who can make optimal use of the suite. They stress recruiting better qualified middle management to run a facility, cross-train employees, provide pay incentives for good performance, and encourage the customer to suggest to employees how a customer problem should be resolved. Such a focus stresses employee involvement toward increasing customer satisfaction. The Disney Corporation as well as the Guest Quarters Suite hotels are also known for their quality service and emphasis on the recruiting and training of their employees who specialize in improving hotel properties. Recruiting, training, and striving to reduce employee turnover is a consistent link running through successful companies. However, as employment figures remain strong and competition for the better trained employees increases, successful recruiting will become more problematic. There is an interesting, indirect method for attracting potential employees that is being successfully used by some of the better service companies in the travel business. They promote their service ethic through community-service affairs, indirectly attracting service-minded potential employees, those who possess a volunteer spirit of helping their fellow citizen in need of community help. The message is equally effective for Delta Airline personnel who recycle aluminum cans or gather unused snacks from flights for distribution through a local food bank. These practices send a goodwill message about the heart of a company and its people.

Labor requirements, where highly skilled employees are required, necessitate that customer service be extremely scheduled in order to maximize work output. The airline industry, for example, unlike others in the travel sector, requires highly skilled, specialized employees who, because of their designated roles, make cross-training impossible (Davidow and Uttal, 1989, p. 150) except for Southwest Airlines that succeeds in certain circumspect situations on the front line. The airline industry is locked into fixed labor costs. To offset that labor constraint, airlines appeal to potential travelers by offering travel incentives such as reduced fares for off-peak hours and advanced booking of reservations. This levels out the demand especially for recreational travel so that highly specialized personnel can be more effectively utilized. The computer-based scheduling of flight crews, the reconfiguring of schedules, class allocation of ticket sales, and knowledge of what class and where the passenger is in route all result in an extremely small percentage of commercial U.S. planes idle at any one time. Most modern airlines have a "big room" where computers and technicians wage a game with weather and breakdowns and have to anticipate options geared toward getting the passenger to a destination "on time." Six tetrabytes of data fly around the American Airlines computer network in a given moment to keep the passenger moving and satisfied. The U.S. General Accounting Office notes that finalists in the prestigious Malcolm Baldridge Award all enjoy improved employee relationships that possess the capability of being responsive. Because a satisfied employee has a better chance of delivering a satisfied customer on time, tourist companies need a stable and trained employee staff whose passion is serving the customer.

External Customers

The external customer is the reason for a tourist business: without customer support and continued satisfaction, there is no business. To keep up with the demands and expectations of a customer, a company has to listen and act upon a customer's judgments, attitudes, and sentiments. The voice of the customer is heard through an interview process that never stops; otherwise satisfaction of the customer may cease. For a "world-class company," communication and feedback from the customer are ongoing, multidimensional, and solicited. Customer input is basically the responsibility of the total organization, and service is defined by continuous improvement based on customer data (Labovitz, Chang, and Rosansky, 1993, p. 31). A few examples from the airline industry that must manage for both business and pleasure customers illustrate how vital such information can be for fulfilling customer needs.

Swissair "asks thousands of passengers several times each year what they think of the airline, and isn't satisfied with an approval rating of less than 96 percent" (Lele and Sheth, 1991, p. 45). The management of Swissair believes it can maintain a competitive position in the airline market by offering "outstanding service" and pays the price of increased fuel consumption to maintain on-time schedules. It has even reconfigured the loading of food and beverage galleys to accommodate the cultural preferences of their passenger mix (Lele and Sheth, 1991, pp. 52, 71, 134). Other airlines possess equally fervid and ambitious programs. Each week, for example, Delta Airlines surveys the previous week's passengers on a variety of subjects to maintain close contact with their passengers on a variety of service-related issues. If an organization is committed to researching and understanding their customer, they must be intent upon implementing that information to better satisfy the wishes of their future passengers. This kind of corporate interest in the customer leads to six key policies shared by all successful service-oriented companies:

(1)　They set themselves impossibly high customer standards.

(2) They are obsessive about knowing what their customers want.

(3) They create and manage customers' expectations.

(4) They design their services to maximize customer satisfaction.

(5) They use financial resources to achieve customer satisfaction.

(6) All divisions in the company have satisfaction as a goal. (Lele and Sheth, 1991, p. 55)

As an unanticipated consequence, the data-gathering process also helps create satisfied customers, and not only provides necessary information, but promotes policies that are geared toward customer service "perfection." This goal is not achievable in a real world, but one that keeps a company doggedly striving to ever improve their customer standing. It is no accident that out of the seven criteria comprising the Malcolm Baldrige Award, the largest point concentration, 30%, is based on satisfying customer expectations.

Information input and opinions from customers form the foundation for improving satisfaction. As such, customer observations are often harshly critical. For the most part, the external customers are most often a rewarding source of interaction and satisfaction for the employee, but they are also a source of irritation when customers dictate to employee. However, if evaluative behavior coming from the customer is part of a routine review process, it becomes institutionalized and normal. The Marriott regularly shares customer assessments with its employees. Such a practice also gets the customer more involved with the goal of quality service and not just the employee (Schneider and Bowen, 1995, pp. 101-105). Such an active role for the customer expands the sometimes narrow definition of a passive recipient. An involved role is especially important when service breaks down or fails the customer.

CUSTOMER SERVICE FAILURES

Measuring Complaints

Customer "no service" is becoming somewhat of a commonplace cliché. In an increasing service-oriented society problems arise simply because of the sheer volume of service. De Rosa (1994, p. 139) notes a growing pessimism toward the marketplace, citing national public opinion polls showing that Americans believe both the quality of products and services is declining and will continue to decline. The pervasiveness of such a negative cloud overshadowing transactions may be increasing, but that is not translating into customers becoming more vocal about bad service. To the contrary, Cannie and Caplin (1991, p. 16) and Barsky (1995) both cite a U.S. Consumer Affairs Report that found 96% of unhappy customers do not complain to management, but they tell an average of 10 other potential customers. Out of the 4% who complain, only half of those whose problem is resolved will remain a customer. The report paints a grim picture of establishments that dissatisfy customers. Since only four out of 100 who experience bad service will report it, there must be a perceived sense of futility to griping. Hinton and Schaeffer (1994, pp. 79-80) do in fact report that customers simply do not complain because "it is not worth the hassle," they don't believe complaining will do any good, they don't know where or how to complain, and finally "people fear retaliation or revenge" if they do complain. Because of this general malaise toward complaining, Davidow and Uttal (1989, p. 15) discount, but do not dismiss, complaints from dissatisfied customers because they represent such a tiny minority of the market. In general, 91% of those having a bad experience will not come back and they will continue to tell other people long after the incident (Cottle, 1990, p. V). As a standard course of action, companies should encourage their customers "to report their problems," but the company should also quickly respond to customer complaints, otherwise they fail the customer twice. Since many customers are reluctant to complain for fear of a confrontation, "customers checking out of the Harvey Hotel in Plano, Texas, may be approached by a 'lobby lizard,' a manager who asks, 'How can we do better?' This opens a less threatening avenue for dialogue and diffuses a potentially negative unreported attitude" (Berry et al., 1993, pp. 9-11). Most of the time, the reasons for disliking a firm may have nothing to do with the price, product, or kind of service. "The good or bad experience is almost always related directly to an experience with people, either attitude or service" delivery (Cottle, 1990, p. 245). The manner of delivery involving the frontline employee often makes or breaks the quality of a service.

In most hierarchically structured organizations, the voice of the customer and the directives of top management meet at middle management's office. Middle management is faced with the risk of resolving customer complaints and taking action that may not be within their organizational sphere of authority. Lytle (1993, p. 33) observes that "more than ever before, our organizations require people to step forward and take customer satisfaction risks. If we simply maintain the status quo, customer dissatisfaction will continue to rise at an alarming rate." Companies often "fail to give employees the flexibility and freedom to use their own common sense in situations where time and creativity are required to satisfy customers" (Lytle, 1993, p. 38). Companies must improve their employees' performance in every frontline situation. When alerted to a problem, Berry and Parasuraman (1991) and Barsky (1995, p. 41) collectively agree on the same checklist to follow in problem situations with customers: foster a positive employee attitude, give access to someone in authority to solve the problem, call with a promised update, understand how the problem happened, offer a solution to the problem and a time frame for it to happen, give progress reports on the solution, tell how it will be prevented in the future, and give alternatives and sufficient diffusing information if no solution can be found. The Ritz-Carlton approach is simple and direct: if you receive a complaint, you "own it," and a timely resolution is mandated. Every incidence of dissatisfaction is communicated within the organization so that employees are empowered to act to resolve and prevent future occurrences.

Despite the small percentage of customers who complain, they tend to hold power and status. They may be small in numbers, but they are not limited in influence. The upper-income and better educated customer is more likely to complain.

In a survey of hotel guests in a northeastern city, complainers indicated that two out of three times they mentioned the complaint to friends and associates, and nearly half said they would caution others not to use the facility (Lele and Sheth, 1991, pp. 213, 216-217). The first problem complainers have is that "nobody really listens to them," so listen sympathetically to the complaint (Cottle, 1990, pp. 249-253). Avoid blaming others, avoid using negative terms like "problem," remain open and non-defensive, focus on a mutually agreed solution, but be careful about quickly offering a fee reduction since it might set an unwarranted precedent, and remember to follow up on a mutually agreed solution, for it strengthens customer credibility in the company (Cottle, 1990, Ch. 17). In the end, be advised that "disenchanted customers can be satisfied if the company acts with speed and dispatch" (Mahfood, 1993, pp. 54, 79). Treat irate customers, not as you would want to be treated, but as they want to be treated. It is their expectations, not yours, that are setting the standards for judging the service performance.

Restoring Service

Despite all the good intentions of service personnel, breakdowns and accidents happen in daily practice. Since it is a good chance such experiences that threaten tourist satisfaction will occur, it is most prudent to preplan for such unfortunate events. "Empirical evidence observed across a variety of service industries indicates that customers who have experienced problems with service suppliers are often dissatisfied with the ways in which problems are resolved" (Spreng, Harrell, and Mackoy, 1995, p. 15). Statistics are presented that indicate the rate of satisfaction with resolving an initial problem ranged between a low of 30% to a high of 67%, leaving on average approximately half of the customers further dissatisfied. That is a double impact on a business's reputation that circulates through word of mouth, causing even further damage. Not enough can be said for turning a negative situation into an immediate positive one.

Every service organization, no matter how good they are in delivering service, must plan for the "handling of poor service." Each organization must prepare a set of "service-recovery policies" enabling the frontline employee to respond to problems with ready-made options to turn a dissatisfied customer into a satisfied client. "Service policies and procedures that address compensating consumers for a lengthy wait, complimentary upgrades if core performance is inadequate, or engendering contact employees to make satisfying customers a priority can often go beyond a customer's expectations" (Walker, 1995, p. 12). Such polices take the sting out of an initial bad experience. Because Hill (1992) favors a proactive stance in managing service, the concept of service recovery to remedy service failure is crucial to ensuring satisfaction. Five steps are seen by Hill (1992) as remedies for a breakdown in service:

(1) Begin with an apology irrespective of the situation and who was to blame; the service provider takes full responsibility.
(2) Urgently reinstate service as a way of saying that you have the customer's interest at heart, and will agreeably satisfy him in that situation.

(3) Exhibit empathy as a genuine response of placing yourself in his situation and offering sincere comfort.

(4) Offer a symbolic atonement such as a gift certificate for a service to show the company cares about him.

(5) And finally, follow up by phone or letter with the client to see that everything was handled to his satisfaction.

Cannie (1994, pp. 100-101) also recommends the same set of criteria for reinstating service status. But on the last item, he, like other professionals, points to the Marriott's Camelback Resort in Arizona and their policy for resolving complaints or any problems before their guests leave. All employees are focused on having no guest leave unhappy, and their top middle managers are responsible for follow-ups. They are one of the few five-star or five-demand properties in the United States demonstrating their earned status. If reliability is the linchpin of service delivery, then responsiveness and timeliness are essential for service recovery. The Camelback Resort operates by a TAGS (Total Associates Guest Satisfaction) program that is written multilingually so that all employees can understand (Cannie, 1994, p. 119). The purpose is to mobilize employees in keeping guests happy or satisfied, and obtaining suggestions from guests for improvements. Obviously, they seriously believe in tracking their own progress. Nobody goes away unhappy or dissatisfied because a policy is in place to correct the service breakdowns.

Remedies are not just service attachments, but vital program strategies to be applied in service-recovery situations. As illustrated in the above, recommendations for implementing a service-recovery program are supported by strong empirical underpinnings (Spreng et al., 1995, pp. 19-20). Three steps are suggested to increase the effectiveness of the recovery process. First, customer-contact personnel should be trained in dealing with service failure, and also in resolving a problem to a customer's satisfaction. By giving the frontline employee the training, responsibility, and authority to immediately deal with an issue, the organization demonstrates their sincere concern and avoids a long process of bumping things up to management for approval. Such action is interpreted with favorable responses from customers. Second, a recovery program should make it easy for a customer to complain about poor service, since most individuals are reluctant to voice their concerns for fear of being hassled. "For example, Embassy Suites provides a free stay if the customer is not 100% satisfied, and this is likely to elicit complaints that would not normally be made." Third, companies should provide adequate funding for service recovery since problem resolution ought to be viewed as an opportunity to make improvements in the service and not just a negative cost. To retain a customer, prevent negative word-of-mouth actions, and prevent further loss of real and potential customers, resources must be made available to the employee.

The effectiveness of the service recovery may have a greater influence on the customer than the original service failure, and service personnel who are in contact with the customer are seen as being key facilitators in determining overall satisfaction (Spreng et al., 1995, p. 16). But, the "friendliness from the staff and sincere apologies do not compensate for unreliable service. Although most customers will appreciate an apology for deficient service, the apology does not erase the memory of that service. If a pattern of service failure develops, customers conclude the firm cannot be counted on, friendly and apologetic or not" (Berry et al., 1993, p. 6). This is not a zero-sum game of either winning or losing. In reality there are areas of gray where interval distinctions are made by reasonable customers. A greater positive difference can be "felt" by the customer than the negative results of providing an attempted, original unreliable service. "Once a customer experiences a problem and seeks resolution, the performance of the recovery process significantly influences behavioral intentions. The magnitude of this effect demonstrates the key role of this type of complaint handling" (Spreng et al., 1995. p. 19). In examining breakdowns in service resulting in dissatisfaction, service process variables are more important during the recovery attempts. Although "reliability is of foremost concern to customers during initial performance of a service, the process dimensions assume prominence during the recovery stage" (Berry and Parasuraman, 1991, p. 46). The process elements of recovery for service include: the staff's responsiveness in providing an acceptable solution(s), the assurance the staff can be trusted to provide compensation, the empathy of the staff conveying a caring concern for the customer, and some tangible offering(s) to satisfy the customer's need. While it may not replace a lost service, such efforts may engender a newfound respect that will carry over into the future intentions of a customer to remain a client and even recommend the service.

> A service recovery plan is a must policy, not an option.

It is best to avoid problems by always providing a reliable service, but there are some companies that take a more active approach and anticipate problems. Three approaches are mentioned that merit future consideration. First, many of the more successful customer-oriented service companies provide after-sale support. They assist with lost items, provide rapid refunds, and provide status updates on problems (Lele and Sheth, 1991, p. 185). They realize that breakdowns are going to happen but faithfully follow up with the customer after the sale. Many product-oriented companies use this approach, but service companies can also adopt a follow-up service on future bookings, lost and found, toll-free information numbers, invitations to future events at a travel destination, etc. You want to make it easy for the customer to select your service again in the future or at least recommend it to another potential customer. Second, "firms need to collect data not only on customer satisfaction but on customer performance.…Failure to take corrective action will yield customer dissatisfaction," especially if the performance features and designs of a tourist environment are too complex for the average customer to handle (Schneider and Bowen, 1995, pp. 97-99). Getting the television to work in one modern, nationally franchised inn proved very complicated for some customers, since there are three switches controlling the set when actually only one is used by the customers. The custodial help were constantly on the move, turning on what the customers thought were defective sets. This puts the staff in an awkward and time-consuming position, resulting in an added cost that could have been relieved by pre-installation testing. Third and finally, strong after-service data gathering can keep a service company vigilant to change and reprogram disinterest. "When it comes to improving client relations, Balboa Travel is at its very best" (Hinton and Schaeffer, 1994, pp. 208-209). They consistently interact with their customers in four key ways. First, they encourage their customers to return their surveys or feedback forms to monitor what they liked or disliked about a trip. Second, they never forget as an internal customer that the external customer pays their salary. Third, they make good use of information exchanges and seminars involving client interests related to their travel needs. Fourth, they educate customers on how best to deal with their service and how to work together toward achieving their travel goals in a cost-effective and pleasant way. After-service sale relations with a customer have potential for improving a service or making a service recovery process more credible and positive. Although customers are out of sight, they are not out of mind.

CONCLUSION

The predominant point to understand is that "services too are bundles of attributes rendering satisfaction" (Walker, 1995, p. 5). The attributes of service that the customer appreciates are mirror images of what the customer expects. The major motivating force in gap theory is whether customers' expectations have been met and exceeded. Expectations are not just the private, subjective reality of the customer; they can be shaped, molded, and influenced. If a tourist-service provider is not proactively creating expectations for potential clients or within the tourist situation through word or deed, they are not providing an acceptable service.

In the pre-consumptive stage, tangible cues help customers form expectations. Depending upon the hospitality situation, service attributes are likely to assume different levels of significance. In a Canadian study of hotel management, Saleh and Ryan (1991) find that the disconfirmation model embodied in the SERVQUAL model provides a useful approach to compare management's performance and the frontline staff. In comparing service quality variables, satisfaction is highest with the tangible aspects that carried over from the pre-consumptive stage of the service and lowest for the empathic and responsiveness factors. Tangible, physical plant attributes relating to the care and maintenance of rooms are vastly more concrete in appearance and are often the only service attributes displayed in promotional materials, often ignoring the training and preparation of the staff to meet the interpersonal needs of the customer. However, Oh and Parks (1997, p. 40) caution against making hasty direct comparisons with the SERVQUAL model because of modifications in applying the model made by Saleh and Ryan (1991). In the consumptive process, the attributes of the service product and providers dictate how expectations are being influenced while in the post-consumptive process, moving the customer to a "prompt," positive exit functions to close a service but offers the prospect of future opportunities. The stages in the service model mark off three distinct areas of different customer interaction with the tourist-service provider. In understanding how satisfaction emerges, changes in the pre- and post-decision process may affect expectations. Service management "should take into account these changes" (Vezina and Nicosia, 1990, p. 40).

It is acts and processes more than physical attributes that promote a service. Internal customer performance, delivery, and execution are the hallmark of service quality. As Schneider and Bowen (1995, pp. 19-20) remind, "services yield psychological experiences more than they yield physical possessions." How well the internal and external customer function together in an interactive situation will determine in large measure how each is satisfied. Communication between the role players in a service situation tends to keep the parties in harmony with service goals. But if service should break down, then the channels of communication are avenues of service restoration. The attributes most important for restoring service are the process dimensions of empathy, assurance, responsiveness, and finally, receiving some tangible reward or benefit for an inconvenience.

The service quality model explains what core attributes affect a customer's response to a service performance. Expectations are the customer's personal measuring stick against which judgments are made regarding satisfaction or dissatisfaction with a service. Tourism is not a routine purchase, and the customer will be less familiar with a particular travel situation, so expectations will not be very structured. As a result, it is necessary in the pre-consumptive and consumptive stage of a service for the tourist providers to set and establish a positive tone by properly communicating cues and outcomes that a customer should anticipate. Assurance and reassurance help relax and calm a customer so that they are more open to a pleasurable experience. The bottom line is satisfaction, and there should be no other alternative when organizing a quality service experience.

A positive outlook toward life insures life satisfaction.

■ 3

Leisure, Tourism, and Hospitality Satisfaction

WHY LEISURE TIME SATISFACTION?

Life Satisfaction and Leisure

AN IMPORTANT relationship exists between an individual's attitude toward life and leisure participation. A positive outlook toward life insures life satisfaction. Such a disposition is reinforced by the psychological and social interactions of individuals that lead to personal happiness and contentment. In a baseline review of empirical studies, life satisfaction is found to be correlated with measures of positive reinforcement such as self-esteem, and inversely with measures of negative reinforcement such as anxiety, worry, depression, and sadness. Robinson and Shaver (1973, pp. 28-36) also report that "a number of studies point to greater satisfaction among people who are actively involved in a number of leisure-time activities." In general, higher positive feelings are associated with leisure activity despite variability in the types of activity. Some of the highest correlates of overall life satisfaction are the result of internal, subjective determinants such as the amount of fun and enjoyment in personal life activities, an interesting daily life, the amount of time available for leisure, relaxation, and physical exercise as opposed to external attributes such as recreation facilities, weather, and one's job (Andrews and Withey, 1976). The substantive benefits from leisure satisfaction are subjective. In that respect, Beard and Ragheb (1980) define leisure satisfaction as the positive perceptions of feelings, which an individual forms, elicits, or gains as a result of engaging in leisure activities and choices. A scale reflecting the subjective meaning of leisure grew out of that research. This includes the psychological benefits, among them a sense of freedom, involvement, educational stimulation, the social rewards of interacting with others, relaxation and relief from daily stress, the aesthetic experiences that are pleasing, beautiful, and well designed, and finally, physiological benefits that help keep body tone and a sense of feeling fit. In a later study, Ragheb and Tate (1993) also find that a leisure attitude strongly affects satisfaction.

In shifting emphasis away from the psychological to lifestyle variables, J. R. Kelly (1981, p. 2) reports evidence from national surveys indicating that "leisure is one major element in life satisfaction, in one case accounting for more variance than work, marriage, or finances, and in another having about the same influences as work satisfaction." In further examining the work-leisure connection that outlines the parameters of adult life, Tate (1984, p. 254) finds that life satisfaction is most influenced by leisure satisfaction, while the smallest impact resulted from job satisfaction. Participation in leisure activities, or possessing a leisure attitude, facilitates increased life satisfaction. More specific findings are found not only among working individuals, but also among retirees who are a rapidly growing segment of the travel market.

Life satisfaction is found to be a critical factor in a senior citizen's physical, spiritual, and mental well-being (Wynne and Groves, 1995). The primary influence that impacts life satisfaction among these studied senior citizens is participation in leisure activities. Riddick and Stewart (1994) also report that among female retirees, life satisfaction is directly affected by perceived self-health, the ability to plan leisure activities, and leisure activity participation among white female retirees. However, the ability to plan leisure activities is shown to be the strongest predictor of leisure participation for both white and black female retirees. This ability indirectly affects life satisfaction through increased leisure participation. And particularly among females, physical leisure activity is more important for reinforcing life satisfaction (Brown and Frankel, 1993). The influence of travel among the senior generational groups is of growing importance as reflected in the results of a telephone survey of adults 40 years and older by Kelly, Steinkamp, and Kelly (1986, 1987) who again demonstrate the independent contribution of leisure to life satisfaction. Travel and social activity are associated with higher levels of life satisfaction for those aged 65-74, and home-based activity for those aged 75 and over. The travel experience provides an avenue of positive reward for the adult retiree to socialize with others in a nonthreatening context. In a sense, travel functions like a number of coffee breaks rolled together and scheduled back to back. "The post-retirement pattern of leisure appears to be one of attrition rather than an increase in salience. Social interaction with family and friends is always important. For those in the sample who have the financial and health resources to engage in a range of activities, much of their social interaction takes place in the context of travel, cultural, and other types of activity that involve doing something together" (Kelly et al., 1987, p. 197). Travel helps maintain social bonds by increasing social interaction. This results in greater integration of an individual in his primary and secondary social relationships within the family and among friends. Sneegas (1986, pp. 255-256) examines the interrelationship between leisure participation and life satisfaction, and how social competence influences the relationship. Competency in social relations is defined as interpersonal skills that provide reinforcement, the accurate presentation of self to others, and nonverbal communication of attitudes and emotions that combines to facilitate interpersonal relationships. Positive perceptions of social competence are found to influence levels of leisure participation and leisure satisfaction, which in turn contribute to life satisfaction. Taking automobile trips and other leisure travel experiences directly affect leisure satisfaction and indirectly affect life satisfaction. Hollywood's version of a family and their pets visiting a theme park, "Wally World," portrays in comedic relief the struggle of a family traveling cross-country to realize their dream of a family vacation. Such travel requires much social competence to achieve leisure satisfaction, as anyone who has been part of that kind of experience recognizes. Travel takes on a major role in providing a context for the kind of private and public interaction that both formally and informally led to greater socialization.

Life satisfaction and leisure travel for pleasure are also important for a quality of life. Neal, Sirgy, and Uysal (1997) recently examined a possible relationship between life satisfaction, leisure satisfaction, and the effect of travel and tourism. Measuring the satisfaction effects of the Clawson/Knetsch model of pre-trip, in-route, destination, and return-home stages establishes where in the travel process satisfaction or dissatisfaction takes place. The findings demonstrate a positive relationship between life satisfaction and satisfaction with a travel and tourist experience. The relationship is more direct than originally thought, and also is important because leisure satisfaction is found not to be directly related to travel or tourist experiences. Although leisure and life satisfaction are shown to be related in previous research, when a tourist experience

> *An important relationship exists between an individual's attitude toward life and leisure participation.*

is the central focus of the activity, leisure activities may just assume a more secondary role in the whole activity. For example, Ute (1991, p. 41) finds that in examining pull forces in tourist motivation, the most important motivating factors are experiencing interesting and friendly local people, outstanding scenery, a warm and sunny climate, environmental qualities of good stewardship, and receiving a warm welcome. The least important activities are leisure or recreational pursuits, including golf, tennis, casino gambling, snow skiing, and hunting and fishing. In contrast, the top activities participated in are sightseeing, shopping, dining out and sampling local foods, taking pictures, and interacting with locals. However, if a large friendship group is traveling together, then active sports are also more likely to be a central focus of the experience. This is not the case for those traveling alone, as couples, as a family, or in an organized tour group unless the activity is a centerpiece of the tour such as golfing, tennis, hunting or fishing trips, and other such sporting excursions. What is evident from the above empirical results is the central finding that life satisfaction is related to leisure activities, and in particular travel and tourist activities. The consequence of experiencing a satisfying trip is not only important for providing an immediate, positive reward for that leisure experience, but has greater far-reaching consequences in that it affects life satisfaction and a person's quality of life. That finding is most significant and underpins the systems approach taken to understanding why satisfaction is such an important factor in tourism.

An Asset and Systems Approach to Tourism

Tourism is part of a larger system of interacting, complex organizations that include leisure, recreation, hospitality, and travel opportunities. Such a definition of tourism is more system or structural in nature rather than person- or individual-oriented. It considers tourism a sum of its organizational parts, unlike some others that are merely psychologically oriented. The individual tourist is not ignored but considered within a larger environmental and situational context that is as large as the world, and as small as a hotel room. In a review of tourist systems, the simplest system according to Uysal (1998) consists of a destination and an origin. This system identifies a destination as a function of supply and the origin with demand. Accordingly, the supply side is divided into three subsystems or assets. The first consists of tourism-oriented products including accommodations, food service, transportation, travel agencies and tour operators, recreation and entertainment, and other travel-trade services. The second is comprised of resident-oriented products that include hospitals, shops and stores, community services, and local establishments for maintaining a viable community life. The third is background tourism elements including the natural, social-cultural, and man-made attractions that frequently constitute some of the main reasons for travel. Tourist demand, however, is influenced by motivational factors, lifestyle, and social demographic characteristics associated with the traveler. Together, according to Uysal (1998), they function in tourist space where the tourist (the demand) travels to the attraction (the tourist product) offered by the tourist industry (the supplier) using the transportation and communication mediums, which provide the essential linkage between demand and supply.

In essence, a tourist system can be viewed as a set of interrelated complex organizational entities that function together to offer a tourism service. They are interdependent upon each other in order to succeed. The organizational units needed to provide the service are comprised of travel assets. The model of tourism used as a guide in understanding satisfaction involves travel assets or organizations that are available to potential pleasure travelers. In that vein, Smith (1994) presents a cogent argument characterizing tourism as an industry that possesses a generic product, process, and experience. "The function of the generic product is the facilitation of travel and activity of individuals away from their usual home environment." The product is comprised of five elements:

(1) A physical plant including the tangible characteristics and conditions of a site (natural setting, buildings, equipment, property, etc.);

(2) Service involving the kind and quality of personnel that maintain and provide for customer needs;

(3) Hospitality involving the responsive dispositions and attitudes of the internal customer (personnel) in offering sincere, empathic service;

(4) Freedom of choice comprising a range of activity options that the tourist is able to voluntarily select;

(5) Involvement of the tourist in rewarding experiences.

"Involvement for pleasure travelers means playing or relaxing in a way that is personally satisfying, and feeling sufficiently safe and secure that one can doze poolside, stroll on the beach, or strike up conversation with other tourists or locals." Such involvement, "combined with freedom of choice, warm hospitality, competent service, and a good physical plant (which includes accessibility, acceptable environmental quality, good weather, and appropriate numbers of people) virtually guarantees a quality and satisfying tourism product" (Smith, 1994, pp. 582, 590-591). This researcher's perspective primarily builds on Gunn's (1988) earlier work asserting that a tourism product is fundamentally a complex human experience that is an integrated process of information, transportation, accommodation, attractions, and services. Whatever provides significant value to the customer in a tourist experience constitutes part of a travel asset.

An asset approach to tourism must involve identifying the major and minor elements that contribute value to a tourist choice. In characterizing the merits of a tourist experience, the public's values are associated with various modes of travel. Such values are compared by Tan and Kundrat (1976), who find that for transportation, automobiles are associated with comfort, family security, and social recognition, while bus riders are seen to value equality but not pleasure. Values are also associated with other modes of travel such as walking, bicycling, and motorcycling. The importance of assigning worth to a tourist experience also includes the whole range of assets associated with a travel situation. These include hotels, restaurants, shops, and the destination, including things to see and buy, the climate and physical surroundings, and the attitudes toward service by the local people toward tourists. Such an enumeration of assets provides the demand side of an equation, which stimulates the interest in the population to travel, and also provides the supply side including major complex organizations that provide information and promotion, transportation, attractions, and services. "The major power unit of the supply side is the attraction component that serves two functions—drawing power and visitor satisfactions" (Gunn, 1990, p. 6). Each component of a travel experience is differently valued by the tourist and contributes to a satisfying or dissatisfying evaluation. A supply side emphasis is concerned about how satisfaction is achieved through the basic interrelated and interdependent organizations. As a step toward understanding the contribution of travel assets to satisfaction, the tourism, hospitality, and recreation literature is reviewed and evaluated with respect to what is empirically reported about influencing customer satisfaction.

EVALUATING A SYSTEM OF TOURISM SATISFACTION

Travel Satisfaction

The social, cultural, and economic significance of tourism projects a positive, ever-upward trend. Burnaby, Swart, and Gearing (1975) envision changes in leisure time that continue to increase both weekend and vacation time through to the year 2000. Continued increases in free or leisure time produce significant consequences for tourism. As Ethridge notes (1982, p. 109) "the cost of a trip is also relative to the leisure time for travel; the greater the leisure time, the greater the likelihood of pleasure travel." Some analyses decry the harried pace of life and work in the United States. Robinson and Godbey (1997) have longitudinally traced the time-budget use of 10,000 survey participants over 30 years. They find that Americans possess more free time than at any point in the past three decades. In contrast with many foreign countries, however, U.S. workers still do not earn as many vacation days, nor reduced hours from shorter work weeks. The end result is relative but still results in more leisure free time for Americans when compared to the past. In the mid-'70s, Kahn (1976) of the Hudson Institute predicted that by the turn of the century in 2000, tourism would be one of the largest, if not the most expansive, industries in the world to absorb some of that free time.

Many possibilities exist for satisfaction and dissatisfaction given the sheer size of the world's market growth and scope. In projecting tourism growth to the year 2000, Edgell (1993, pp. 64-70) also finds signs that "international tourism, in fact, is likely to grow more rapidly than the U.S. economy as a whole and will become increasingly important in the international sector of the U.S. economy." The implications are not only economic but also sociocultural because of greater international contact with tourists. As a consequence, "there will be more cosmopolitanism and less provincialism in the sense that traveling widely will be the expectation of great numbers of people, and little of the world will be totally unknown or unfamiliar." The economic numbers are impressive. "In the year 2000, the worldwide tourism industry (domestic and international) which is today the largest sector, generating over $2 trillion in receipts, will continue to be the largest sector and its receipts will double to at least 4 trillion." Estimates of international travelers will increase to 67 million in the year 2000 in comparison to 40 million just a decade earlier (Edgell, 1990, pp. 32, 34). Demographics will also play a big part with the over-'50s generation; showing the greatest increase in the travel market accompanying this will be a new concern for diet, health, and more exercise that leads to a better quality of life and longer longevity. The Elderhostel programs, which continue to grow and expand throughout the world, are examples of providing older adult learners with enriching experiences. The interests of these potential travelers must be reflected in the programs and services offered by the hospitality industry if they are going to satisfy this market segment. Interests are created or popularized by promoters for tourists. There is no set of innate, intrinsic interests that motivate the tourist to be satisfied, especially when commercial opportunities are at stake where a market can be exploited. McCartney reports (1997) that the fastest growing tourist segment comprises people aged 45 to 64. This segment is expected to increase 16% over the next five years and includes people who may be attracted to places such as Graceland in Memphis, Tennessee, since they were Elvis fans in their youth. Hard Rock, Motown, and Planet Hollywood cafes promote spending a week "hanging out with the rockers," a kind of institutionalized Grateful Dead experience but more Wall Street polished. Theme park cafes that appeal to tourists are developing a niche along theme park lines. This attraction serves two functions: drawing power and fulfilling satisfaction needs. The travel industry continues to develop new demographic markets spanning all age generations and creates points of interest to attract those markets. As a result, tourism is "more of an escape-oriented" response. As such, "tourism is more likely to be triggered by the escape motive because of the travel industry's constant promotion of the need to escape over- or under-stimulating everyday environments" and "a trend toward more frequent, but shorter, vacations suggest[s] that the escape dimension is a more important motivation" (Mannell and Iso-Ahola, 1987, p. 328). The form that escapism takes may be changing, as a Lou Harris poll (1992) reports for *Travel and Leisure* magazine, from one of luxury and spending money freely to more cultural and enriching activities. Whatever the motivation, modern tourism has taken a big step toward global involvement and promises to be even a bigger part of modern-day lifestyles in the future. The role of the tourist has also changed.

Tourist Role

A tourist is defined as a person "away from home to the extent that their behavior is motivated by leisure related factors" (Leiper, 1990, pp. 371-2). In addition, the work of other experts is summarized by Leiper (1990) noting that the tourism-leisure connection involves five structural elements. First, "the essence of touristic behavior involves a search for satisfying leisure away from home. Second, tourist leisure means a search for suitable attractions or, to be more precise, a search for personal (*in situ*) experience of attraction systems nuclear elements 'that can be expressed as lists of what tourists might want to experience.' A far more common condition is that each tourist is involved with a range of nuclei or characteristics of interest. Third, the travel experience depends ultimately on each individual's mental and non-mental attributes, such as needs and ability to travel. Fourth, the markers (sources of information) are informative elements that have a key role in the links between each tourist and those nuclear elements being sought for personal satisfying experiences. Fifth, the process is not automatically productive, because tourists needs are not always satisfied." The collective purpose of these five characteristics is simply to enhance satisfaction. These five characteristics also stress the importance of the structural elements of a travel experience but not the subjective process.

In taking a more process perspective, a tourist is defined by Cohen (1974, p. 533) as "a voluntary, temporary traveler, traveling in the expectation of pleasure from the novelty and change experienced on a relatively long and nonrecurrent or rarely undertaken round trip." A large part of the pleasure gained from a trip is the satisfaction with destination facilities, services, and programs. In an earlier work on the sociology of tourism, Cohen (1972, p. 165) believes that the value of novelty about a new experience that excites a tourist is "possible only when man develops a generalized interest in things beyond his particular habitat, when contact with and appreciation and enjoyment of strangeness and novelty are valued for their own sake." This seems to be a thoroughly modern phenomenon. However, tourists also value the familiar. Zalatan (1994, p. 9) tests the premise that "satisfaction with the trip is largely explained by *ex ante* variables, that is, variables which are predetermined before the tourist heads to his destination." A crucial *ex ante* variable defining this type of customer/tourist interaction is familiarity. According to Zalatan (1994, p. 11) "familiarity would tend to reduce uncertainty and increase tourist satisfaction. For years, the success of the Holiday Inn was reflected in their slogan 'The best surprise is no surprise.' While the tourist expects novelty and discovery, his previous knowledge of the destination would only enhance his satisfaction." Cohen (1972, p. 167-172) links the novel and the familiar at either end of a tourist continuum. The "organized mass tourist" anchors one end who is the "least adventurous" where "familiarity is at a maximum." At the other extreme lies the least institutionalized, "the drifter," who seeks the highest degree of adventure by being "farthest from the beaten track," where novelty is at its highest, and familiarity disappears. "The experience of tourism combines, then, a degree of novelty with a degree of familiarity, the security of old habits with the excitement of change." In appealing to the mass tourist, "made necessary by the difficulties of managing and satisfying large numbers of tourists, the attributes of a destination tend to be simplified, catalogued, and sometimes even assigned a level of importance" by the travel agent. As the wider appeal of tourism becomes formally institutionalized on a mass level of appeal, the qualities of novelty, strangeness, and variety disappear. The range of expectations is also at a minimum and the risk of surprising a tourist with a service that may change expectations is less likely for fear of causing dissatisfaction. By far, mass tourists are conservative in role and expectations. They expect the ordinary and are not disappointed by it. When surprises are effectively planned, they are usually extraneous of existing expectations that boost satisfaction.

The theme of a tourist experience is not singular in character. Cohen (1979) describes a range of tourist experiences along an ideal-type continuum beginning with the recreational and ending with existential types of travel. The recreational type is considered the most superficial, motivated by the desire for mere pleasure. Recreational tourism is not a serious business but rather an idle pleasure that gains recognition on the strength of its recuperative powers for the overworked modern traveler. At the other end of the continuum is the existential tourist who seeks a highly authentic cultural experience by voluntarily separating himself from his own culture and participating as a surrogate in a foreign culture. Many pilgrims or enthusiasts of a cultural interest fall into this category of tourist. Neither extreme of experience is any less real, nor is it inconceivable for a tourist to combine elements of these two extremes into a single trip. Depending on the type of desired trip, tourists' "expectations will change depending on the level of novelty and the type of experience being sought." Egan (1976) provides actual case illustrations examining studies in a historical perspective on the development of tourist destination and the interface between recreation and cultural tourism. In the prewar days, Hawaii is seen as being completely recreational, including swimming, beach activity, and boating. As of 1946, only 1500 hotel rooms existed and a good portion needed refurbishing after military use. Recognizing the beauty of the natural and cultural resources, Hawaiians organized the resources into parks, beach resorts, garden clubs, and cultural events to attract interested tourists. American Samoa and the Antalya area in Turkey along the Mediterranean also illustrate where the recreational and cultural resources are organized so as not to destroy the natural resources, but provide safeguards to the environment and cultural heritage. National park designations or historical preservations are most effective in controlling excessive commercial speculation. Such an approach recognizes that the recreational and cultural process is important in controlling travel outcome. Tourism is a complex collection of organizations and interests

> *The social, cultural, and economic significance of tourism projects a positive ever-upward trend.*

dealing with managed tourist development. In this sense, "recreation and tourism can be considered as separate systems with many interrelated parts. But they are subsystems of a larger system which is the total environment in which they operate" (Egan, 1976, p. 10). Recognizing the mix of recreational, cultural, and natural area attributes of tourism opens up more possibilities for exciting expectations.

The Tourism Expectancy Model

In marketing profiles, social economic status variables (SES) and demographic customer characteristics usually assume a center-stage position in describing or attempting to predict tourist expectations. However, Zalatan (1994) is of the opinion that for many people a trip is the fulfillment of a dream. And dreams are often the fruit of our imagination. The results of Zalatan's study reveal that adult tourists have higher satisfaction if the following hold true. (1) The destination is in line with their desires (congruence). (2) They are more familiar with the destination country. The behavioral variables of congruence between expectations, outcome, and familiarity with the destination are statistically more salient or important. Because of this finding, "a strong linkage between expected satisfaction and actual satisfaction" is suggested (Zalatan, 1994, p. 9). As a consequence, it is not surprising that, in many cases, there is a gap between the actual trip and the trip as initially envisaged by the tourist. How congruent or incongruent our expectations and perceptions of a travel situation may become in turn affect the outcome of a satisfaction level. As previously noted, routine purchases are probably more apt to be affected by comparisons, but they are also affected by information, advertisements, and word-of-mouth accounts that inexplicably shape expectations.

The expectancy standards of comparison that make sense of everyday decisions facilitate judgments in a tourist context. Leiper (1990, pp. 371, 380) analogously uses the language of physics in defining the element of a human-tourist, a nucleus, or list of characteristics that a tourist expects to experience. In fact, social markers lead the way for the tourist by providing sources of information about the destination, activities available, names, connotations about the sites, itinerary planning, and items of interest. However, tourists are not "magnetically" pulled to an attraction but rather pushed by their own motivation "towards the places and or events they expect will satisfy their needs." Tourists expect a quality experience and to be satisfied. Pizam (1991) observes "that quality in tourism is the consumer-rated ability of a product or service to satisfy consumer needs as compared to expectations. It is a subjective overall measure reflecting several characteristics of the product/service that is valued by the consumer." The characteristics of tourism service quality are distinguished by the following:

(1) Quality is not inherent in the properties of the service itself but is a function of the tourist's values which govern expectations and perceptions.
(2) Quality perceptions result from a comparison of their expectations with actual service performance.
(3) Quality evaluations are not made solely on the outcome of a service; they also involve evaluations of the process of service delivery.
(4) Quality perception is subjective and has to be seen through the tourist's eyes and not the eyes of managers of the tourism organization.
(5) Quality requirements will be different for various tourist segments.
(6) Quality perception is influenced by the tourist's needs, values, previous experience, situation, and many other factors.
(7) Quality perceptions are dynamic and change over time. This model is an exact copy of what has evolved from past research as already summarized in the two previous chapters. Research applications, though few in number in the scientific literature, follow upon this service-quality orientation.

In a study of visitor expectations of tourism benefits in Zambia, Husbands (1994) finds that the tourists studied "do not anticipate a highly complex product; visitors anticipate and expect that Zambia offers fewer benefits." The attribute coincides with what the tourist found most satisfying, namely viewing wildlife, scenery, and experiencing African culture. Night life, diversity of attractions, and hotel kinds of accommodations are viewed as least important to a stay. The findings are consistent with the earlier suggestion concerning the generally low level of diversification of the Zambian tourism product. "Those dissatisfied, however, tended to place higher demands and expectations on the Zambian experience regarding opportunities for local travel, experiencing the local cuisine, and visiting cultural areas of interest; these attributes of the experience generally fell just below the top expectations" (Husbands, 1994, pp. 35-36). Tourists who stayed for a longer period tended to be dissatisfied with the lack of options and opportunity to fulfil some of the above expectations. Given the many options in today's world, expectations will vary by destination but also by market segment. In one such study measuring the evaluational responses of budget-oriented travelers who took into consideration the expectations for enjoyment, Ross (1993, p. 478) finds more positive evaluations come from less educated, younger males who seldom take vacations. However, less favorable judgments come from better educated females who take regular vacations and whose experiences are less than what was expected as enjoyable. Research is cited that finds that an expectancy model is a "powerful predictor in any evaluation of a tourism venue or destination." In another comparison of American escorted tourists, who are largely female with a median age between 66-70, Duke and Persia (1994) find significant differences in expectations between foreign and domestic tours. The foreign tourist possesses higher expectations for tour comfort and value, along with the need for adequate stops to see what is important, and seek adventure and educational rewards. In addition, the foreign group expected to get their money's worth, to be safe, to enjoy a friendly group atmosphere, and to experience enjoyable tour guides. These kinds of expectations are where "firms must compete on what-ever level of issues that are not yet met." Both the domestic and foreign tour groups expect comfort, scenery, and experienced tour guides, but those traveling to a "for-eign" destination possess relatively higher expectations.

Factors causing shifts in travel or vacation expectations might also be the re-sult of more extrinsic influences. Occupations and work are a central life interest in modern society and are considered a powerful social force. Individuals satisfied with their work usually gain more pleasure in their leisure. "This means that the value also of leisure will be greater to those who enjoy their work than those who do not" (Scitovsky, 1992, p. 104). In measuring the work influence, however, no sig-nificant relationship is found between work experience variables such as job satis-faction, involvement, the pace and physical activity of the work, role conflict or ambiguity at work, and overall vacation satisfaction (Lounsbury and Hoopes, 1985).

Interpersonal relations are yet another extraneous variable like work that may affect expectations and satisfaction. In a European cross-cultural comparative study of family decision making regarding vacations, Seaton and Tagg (1995, pp. 15, 17) examine the role of children in vacation decision making and the relationship be-tween these roles and vacation preferences. A sample of children and parents from Italy, Belgium, France, and the UK are included. The findings show that there is a strong relationship between expressed satisfaction and post-decisional approval. Over 80% of the children who had approved the decision expressed the highest levels of satisfaction versus 33.1% who had not approved. Although there are some small differences between countries in specific vacation outcome response, satisfactions are comparable across countries and families. A range of intrinsic and extraneous variables such as work and interpersonal relations are likely to affect expectations and satisfaction as the few empirical studies published to date report.

Tourism studies also demonstrate that expectations are molded by informa-tion sources either through the printed mass media or word of mouth. Larsson

(1994) reports that tour operators communicate promises of social relations, excitement, and adventure. Images are also molded and colored by tourist societies. While on the tour, it is the guide who plays a key role in promoting tourist satisfaction. But the impersonal media also play a role. Cooper (1994) examines how tourist images are communicated through promotional travel brochures, guide books, maps, and postcards to manipulate the tourist experience. These sources of information diffusion produce mental images that give a tourist's journey social justification. Information gives credence to modern leisure activities associated with travel and is a major contributor of tourist expectations.

Leisure activities also help shape tourist expectations. "There is a need to identify leisure factors such as vacations which account for variations in the level of tourist satisfaction without specific reference to a particular site" (Zalatan, 1994, pp. 9-10). A satisfaction rating reflects the "voluntary and free dimensions of a vacation." Individuals are probably more satisfied with leisure than other obligatory facets of life and a vacation is viewed by many as "a direct source of satisfaction." Because many vacations involve travel and recreation activities, it is important to more fully examine what affects satisfaction. Lounsbury and Hoopes (1985, pp. 9-10) find that satisfaction is strongly associated with leisure and relaxation and accounts for 53% of the explained variance in overall vacation satisfaction. Seven attributes describe the leisure-relaxation attributes. They include:

(1) the way one's plans or expectations work out,
(2) the way a person feels emotionally,
(3) the way a person feels physically,
(4) the "pace-of-life" experienced,
(5) opportunities to engage in favorite leisure activities,
(6) opportunities to engage in new leisure activities, and
(7) the amount of relaxation experienced.

These subjective attributes lead the researchers to conclude that "vacation satisfaction might be highly subjective and not predictable from objective attributes of either people or situations. If vacation satisfaction is a joint function of a person's own individual needs, tastes, desires, and expectations on the one hand, and the actual vacation experiences on the other, one can see that there would be many different ways to realize (as well as not realize) a satisfying vacation." Such findings and conclusions parallel those on life satisfaction where "internal subjective" attributes are viewed as stronger predictors than external attributes.

Recreation-Leisure Role

Recent recreation research seems to reinforce the concept that leisure satisfaction is a multidimensional concept encompassing many different recreational groups (Herrick and McDonald, 1992, pp. 243-246). In a sample of recreational river users, including floaters, rafters, and kayakers, differences explained in satisfaction included group behavior, setting characteristics, perceived crowding, parking, encounters with other river users, and past experience. Twenty-one percent of the variance in satisfaction was explained by how well the rafters interacted, or how well they evaluated the tangible attributes of the river setting. The remaining 10% of the explained variance was explained by the availability of parking, encounters with other river users, perceived crowding, and past user experience. Different types and mixes of variables in other recreation situations also affect satisfaction. In a survey of camper satisfaction, for example, Connelly (1987, pp. 165-170) presents data that show feelings of solitude and rejuvenation, an interest in nature (the plants, wildlife, scenery), and clean and litter-free facilities being positively associated with a satisfying camping experience. In terms of the statistical analysis, the feelings associated with rejuvenation, relaxation, being dissociated from crowds and daily problems are seen as being part of a more universal, personal perception of a situation, whereas perceptions of nature and the facilities are more dependent on particular site and user characteristics. Interestingly, one of the items least associated with camper satisfaction is "seeing tourist attractions." Campers appear to be more site oriented, staying multiple days and taking advantage of the water-based recreation opportunities such as motorboating or canoeing. The two studies demonstrate the influence of a variety of variables, emphasizing situational, psychological, and behavioral attributes that affect satisfaction in a recreational travel experience.

In keeping with a multivariate approach in researching leisure-recreation satisfaction, Riddick (1986, p. 63) classifies attributes of leisure satisfaction into a combination of predisposing factors (age, sex, leisure values, knowledge of leisure resources), reinforcing factors (spouse, mate, or best friend's leisure attitude), and an enabling factor (income). "Quite clearly, of all the variables considered, two predisposing factors (knowledge of leisure resources and leisure values) appear to have a profound influence on leisure satisfaction." Possessing positive leisure values and being informed of leisure choices are subjective channels of opportunity that lead to leisure satisfaction. Other subjective influences also prove to be related to leisure satisfaction. The concept of involvement is an important example. As an internal subjective attribute, involvement is a state of motivation, arousal, or interest produced by a particular stimulus or situation. Two of the most salient dimensions of involvement include the perceived personal importance or relevance, and the hedonic value or emotional appeal to provide pleasure. According to Havitz, Dimanche, and Howard (1993, p. 344), "The importance-pleasure dimension is the first factor to emerge, and it accounted for 50% of the explained variance." In particular, the researchers point out applications in tourism and leisure where importance and pleasure merge. They assert that the notion of a "recreational or touristic experience becomes important because it is pleasurable and has intuitive appeal" (Dimanche, Havitz, and Howard, 1991, p. 62). Pleasurable leisure experiences reinforce a person's satisfaction and positive expectations. Persons with an optimistic attitude toward life perhaps see less discrepancy between their desired and experienced satisfaction with leisure. A study by Francken and van Raaij (1981, pp. 337, 350) explains leisure satisfaction by the discrepancy between the actual and desired situation. "Leisure satisfaction is higher for people who are older and have an optimistic outlook or expectation. They do not perceive a discrepancy between their actual and desired number of hours spent on leisure activities. Persons with low leisure satisfaction tend to be younger and have a pessimistic outlook." Age and expectation combine in part to explain leisure satisfaction in this study. Having an optimistic outlook toward life may also attract more participants to experience leisure satisfaction. In a study of day-use hikers in a national forest just outside of Aspen, Colorado, Hull, Stewart, and Yi (1992, pp. 245-249) find that approximately a little over 40% of the hikers actually enter "the setting feeling very satisfied and stay that way throughout the hike." These hikers' feelings of satisfaction are virtually independent of the attributes of the setting and the internal factors such as fatigue and boredom. When examining the remaining sample of hikers with varying satisfaction levels, a combination of internal and external influences emerges. The internal attribute of boredom depresses satisfaction on the uphill hike, while the external condition of scenic beauty remains significant throughout but is just slightly more important on the downhill leg of the hike. Internal and external or subjective and situational factors in a person's leisure experience combine to explain satisfaction. Other studies, too, demonstrate the interplay of multivariate attributes, sometimes tending more toward the subjective and other times more toward the situational or group behavioral attributes. The recreational activity itself also combines to interact in an explanation of satisfaction.

Vaske, Donnelly, Heberlein, and Shelby (1982, pp. 196-198, 203) argue that satisfaction is derived from the interaction between individual characteristics and the characteristics of the activities. Recreation is classified along a continuum, from consumptive recreational activities that provide participants with products, to non-consumptive that provide experiences. Non-consumptive activities are multifaceted and the goals are more diffuse and general, unlike consumptive recreation activities such as hunting or fishing whose focus on the core activity is narrow. A non-consumptive recreation experience might include a trip, picnic, or bicycle ride as a single experience. A tourist trip is an excellent example of a non-consumptive activity. Such activities provide a measure of control over option selections during the experience with perhaps more foresight about what to expect. These participants have greater assurance over successfully fulfilling their expectations, whereas consumptive users have no assurance that the hunt will produce game or fish. As a result, "these data show that across a wide variety of geographic areas and recreation populations, those who engage in a non-consumptive activity report higher levels of overall satisfaction than those who engage in a consumptive activity." Assurance may be easier to obtain in a non-consumptive pleasure activity. But even in consumptive activities, rigid distinctions cannot be made. Buchanan (1983, pp. 46-48) finds that among the top factors that affect satisfaction in a survey among recreational fishermen are catching fish, relaxing, reducing stress, resting physically, escaping personal-social pressures, socializing with friends, or being with family. In fact, the secondary recreational activities, such as visiting with others, going to town, relaxing and sitting around a campfire, or going for a walk, are also linked to satisfaction in a travel situation. In one consumptive situation, the attributes actually reversed importance. For a sample of goose hunters in a highly managed situation in Vermont, the importance of the resource demonstrates how changes dramatically shift when the circumstances change. Unlike other hunter satisfaction surveys, the most important motives or satisfactions related in this situation are being with friends, enjoying the natural environment, relaxing and relieving tensions, feeling excitement, and nostalgia or recalling past memories which the situation evoked. Actually, harvesting a goose was ranked in the middle of choices of importance. What distinguishes this hunt from others is a lottery system that is used to select the hunters who can then invite two guests to share the blind. With a limited number of blinds, the hunt becomes even more select. Since chance and luck are a big part of any hunt, the lottery system becomes the main part of the hunt and shifts emphasis to the more social and internal sources of satisfaction (Glass and More, 1992). The highly managed circumstances of this situation change what would be acceptable sources of satisfaction. In other words, the circumstances of limited availability and the lottery shifts expectations regarding the consumptive attribute of the activity. While the multidimensionality of attributes associated with recreational satisfaction varies widely among recreational groups, many of the studies follow a gap or expectance model that is more able to efficiently sort out the significance of the various attributes.

The Recreational Expectancy Model

In using expectations as a predictor, Ditton, Fedler, and Graefe (1981) cluster river floaters into groups according to the similarities in the importance they attach to eight expectations or outcomes about a river trip. Among the groups, overall satisfaction tends to "achieve similar levels of satisfaction"; however, differences between the groups over what predicts that satisfaction range widely. The most important expectations averaged over all the groups range from seeking a change in daily routine, becoming close to nature, seeking thrills and excitement, and being with friends. Fulfillment of the expectation to have thrills and excitement and to experience the pleasure of nature accounts for the most common variance predicting overall satisfaction between the groups. But each group tended to place different emphasis on what interested them; one group placed greater emphasis on being with friends, while another valued thrills and excitement. According to the researchers, "satisfaction means different things to different people." The importance of attribute values, organized by how different groups weigh them, captures the diversity in a population by clarifying what motivates individuals to seek recreational satisfaction. But groups placing different emphasis on expectations is but one factor in how expectations vary. Another relates to the kind of gap in the attributes of expectation that are evaluated within a recreational experience.

Using a gap model to evaluate satisfaction, Shelby, Lowney, and McKee (1980) accept a definition of satisfaction as the perceived discrepancy between aspiration and achievement, ranging from the perception of fulfillment to that of deprivation. In other words, the gap between expectations and perceptions defines a level of satisfaction among attributes. They distinguish between objective and subjective attributes in a variety of social situations such as satisfaction with a community, marriage, job, and recreation. The findings suggest that satisfaction is "usually correlated with subjective perceptions and evaluations but not with objective attributes." In dealing with perceptions of crowding, objective attributes such as a level of overall site use and encounters with other parties contribute only 3% in explained variance. Subjective attributes dealing with perceptions of learning and personal growth add 32% more in explained variance. The crowding model of satisfaction tends to dominate in recreational studies that assume "an inverse relationship between user density and satisfaction." In a review by Manning (1985, pp. 50-76) of studies covering a wide range of outdoor recreational activities on various sites, "considerable doubt is cast on the satisfaction model since density and satisfaction are seemingly so unrelated" in recreation situations. What is of interest are the multiple intervening and confounding factors cited, much like what appears in the service-quality approach. These factors include attitudes and expectations, perceptions of the situation, visitor or customer sensitivity to site design, and the kind of contact between recreation users. These all undermine the simplicity of the original explanation of the model. What this clearly demonstrates is the complex nature of satisfaction where single causative factors are probably not sufficient explanations. However, in an earlier study examining how perceptions of density affect satisfaction, Manning and Ciali (1980, p. 339) find some support for the no-expectations hypothesis that "puts forth the notion that many recreationists, particularly those with little or no experience, have no expectations as to what density levels will be and are generally satisfied with what they find." Density is not a source of dissatisfaction for the first-year river users, while no significant relationship is found for those river recreation users with more years of experience.

In another study, Shelby (1980, p. 50) examines perceptions of crowding and satisfaction among whitewater rafters in Grand Canyon National Park. Forty-nine percent of the variance in perceptions of crowding is accounted for by expectation and feeling variables, following the above predictions of stronger subjective factors. However, despite whitewater rafters expecting to be alone or feeling the area is overused, satisfaction is little affected by these crowding factors. The rafters feel that they learn from the trip and report high satisfaction, as did people who enjoy the social aspects of the experience. In a follow-up study that evaluated a different kind of river user, namely inner-tube floaters on the Hiwassee River in Cherokee National Forest, Hammitt, McDonald, and Noe (1984, p. 7) find that perceptions and more objective attributes such as visual encounters and the actual use level account for 43% of the variance in perceived crowding; less than 4% is explained by feeling and expectations. The researchers account for the difference by the degree of "specialization" needed for Grand Canyon rafting, as opposed to inner-tube floating. Because of the differences in the level of skill required, equipment, and challenge of the resource setting, Grand Canyon raft floaters "formulate more specific expectations and feelings about the appropriate use levels than inner-tube floaters using an everyday river." If the gap model measures expectations and perceptions with respect to satisfaction, then the setting and situation become important depending upon how much skill and knowledge is required to participate in that leisure activity. In many travel situations, specialization skills are usually reserved for a recreational activity such as golf, tennis, fishing, gambling, etc. that accompanies the tourist experience. Kabanoff (1982) also reports that skill utilization contributes to a strong relationship with leisure satisfaction among a stratified sample of employees in Adelaide, Australia. In comparing blue-collar against white-collar workers, lower-status, blue-collar workers are less likely to report skill needs or expectations for leisure pursuits.

In travel situations, where a type of recreation requiring a higher degree of specialization is needed, participants' feelings and expectations are likely to be more specific and focused. In a study of visitors to Cape Lookout National Seashore, Floyd (1993a) reports in detail what is and what is not expected by visitors in evaluating their experience to the outer banks and island. Given the spe-

> The recreational activity itself also combines to interact in an explanation of satisfaction.

cific nature and definition of the sites along the outer banks, very specific site services, facilities, and programs are specified to help to define certain types of expectations. Aveni (1980) notes a similar finding for an event held in an urban recreation area along the Chattahoochee River National Park that attracted many thousands of spectators and participants. Attendees are very pointed about what facilities, services, and programs they found satisfying or dissatisfying. Again, these recreation and travel situations are very specialized in their offerings and in the information made available through brochures and the mass media. Expectations are formed and molded through communication, but there is also an expectation by the tourist for receiving information.

Manning (1985, pp. 6-7) cites a series of studies spanning the 1960s and 1970s that focuses on recreational satisfaction and the "need for some evaluative communication between visitors and managers." Satisfaction depends on visitors and their perceptions as much as on the characteristics of the site. Williams and Patterson (1991) find that forest visitors rank the scenery of the natural area first, followed by reasonable fees, location near residence, helpfulness of the employees, good roads, and parking. Few respondents express dissatisfaction with any of the attributes ranked. However, there are some mixed satisfied/dissatisfied responses with the lack of available information about the area and its history plus responses about program offerings. Information and expectations reinforce each other. In a survey of Canadian West Coast Trails, Rollins and Associates (1993) rate information at the trailheads for hikers as the most satisfying attribute. Using multiple studies of U.S. National Parks from 1988-93, Machlis and Medlin (undated) report that visitors' top-rated services included interacting with rangers, word-of-mouth communication, and information obtained from park brochures. The Moores Creek National Battlefield survey finds that of the top five expectations, four relate to expecting specific kinds of information (Floyd, 1993b). Two out of the top five problems reported relate to inadequate information. Again, the significance of information shows itself as an important, instrumental facilitator of service activity.

In concluding this section, Dorfman's work (1979, pp. 497, 503) is a useful summary study because it exemplifies a very traditional approach to measuring recreation satisfaction. It assesses how the respondents' perceptions, preferences, and expectations affect their levels of satisfaction. The findings suggest that "an individual's overall satisfaction is more dependent upon his/her perception of the conditions deemed valuable; secondarily, it is influenced by the difference between what he/she perceives and would prefer; and least of all, it reflects the differences between what is perceived and what is expected." Discrepancy measures do not correlate as highly as direct measures of perception. This latter finding is not unlike what occurs in the service-quality research. The conclusion reached is somewhat different in that "it probably is more useful to consider the difference between what a person prefers and what he/she finds as an indicator of satisfaction than the difference between what he/she expects and finds. For example, finding a campsite littered with garbage, even if one expected to find it, would result in dissatisfaction with that aspect of the experience." But from a diagnostic point of view, it is necessary to also determine what an expectation holds so that it can be exceeded. Following on the example given, finding no litter would be unexpected and thus exceed the expectancy norm of the campers relating to positive feelings of satisfaction. But that has to be measured to be determined, and measuring preferences alone will not yield that kind of information. In comparing the camper's ratings, Dorfman (1979, pp. 503-507) also finds consistency in the importance and satisfaction associated with attributes. The tangible qualities of a good campsite, the absence of negative conditions, offering opportunities for relaxation, and positive social interaction are rated as important and satisfying to the camper. Despite that pattern, the weighing of attributes by importance did not improve predictions. But the importance measures of an attribute are "indicative of the impact" an attribute will have on overall satisfaction, thus identifying the more valuable attributes. Expectations, perceptions, and valued preferences are part of the leisure-recreational studies explanation of participant satisfaction.

Hospitality Provider Role

Extended and overnight travel requires lodging and food services as part of the experience. It takes the role of a service provider to meet a customer's needs. The most fundamental organizational factor offering the customer a satisfactorily rewarding experience is a satisfied employee. Kirwin (1992, pp. 38-39), vice president of lodging operations for the Carlson Hospitality Group that includes Radisson Hotels International, Colony Resorts and Hotels, and T.G.I. Friday's restaurants, emphasizes the following recommendations to ensure satisfied customers:

(1) focus on hiring happy, outgoing, friendly employees,
(2) recognize and reward staff for good service,

(3) empower the employee to meet guests' needs and resolve problems,

(4) allocate funds for customer-service expenses, and

(5) direct capital outlays to implement customer and guest suggestions which is a call "to start trusting customers."

It is not surprising that the first three recommendations point toward employing a happy frontline support staff that is able to provide a credible service. A hotel in Atlanta, Georgia, that may not be so atypical, reported an annual 300% turnover rate, making it virtually impossible to provide consistency in service quality. The current turnover and attrition of employees in the hospitality industry directly affects customer satisfaction, but this can be reversed by implementing the following solutions (Pizam and Milman, 1990, pp. 14-17). The first is to change the image of the industry from a low paying, dead-end job by being more aggressive in an educational effort to publicize career opportunities. Second, change managerial direction by finding ways to improve employee benefits. Third, pay higher salaries. Fourth, attract nontraditional labor who may be older, downsized, or schooled in other disciplines. Fifth, introduce high-tech features where guests can execute, for example, food choices through self-serve automated food and drink or check out services. Sixth, develop recruiting and marketing campaigns that attract better qualified employees, including giving a "referral fee" to current employees who attract others. And finally, offer multi-ladder career options that vary time and location moves to accommodate the employee. "The problem of labor shortage in the tourism industry will, for the time being, remain a principal issue." That does not imply there are no solutions. Employee incentive, benefit, and reward programs must be examined. Such programs might help insure that employees delivering the organization's service and message will enhance the interests of the organization through positive communication with the customer.

When lapses or breakdowns in hospitality services occur, as they inevitably will, Sparks and Callan (1996, pp. 12, 16) evaluate what type of explanation, offer, and communication style are most effective in restoring the customer's positive assessment of the service provider. An internal explanation and full acceptance of blame by the service provider for the service failure is received most favorably. An offer of compensation is also important for restoring confidence, but an "offer needs to be congruent with the perceived cause of the problem." A service provider who offers true value is perceived as trying harder than one who offers mere symbolic value. Finally, an accommodating style of communication moves closer to the position of the customer. So much transpires between the service provider and customer that interpersonal exchange is the focal point for resolving unmet expectations. It appears that how an offer is communicated is most important for restoring lost confidence. In an earlier investigation of communication styles, Sparks (1994) finds that a convergent style of communication used by hotel reservation personnel is perceived more positively by the customer. "By personalizing the talk of the reservationist, it is likely that the prospective customer will see the reservationist as more accommodating and more effective." Negative connotations result when the reservation personnel are unsure or uncertain about the information being communicated. It is within these types of encounters that "determinants of customer satisfaction-dissatisfaction" are formed. "In summary, customers evaluate the quality of a service, at least in part, on the manner in which information is communicated" (Sparks, 1994, pp. 44-48). Highly involved customers seek out information so it is even more crucial to manage this part of the business process. Involvement is a personal state reflecting the amount of interest, arousal, or emotional attachment an individual puts toward a product or service. It is reported that among active, ethnic-restaurant customers, a consumer's opinions, beliefs, and behavioral intentions are significantly correlated with satisfaction (Ladki and Nomani, 1996, p. 21). An active consumer seeks and spends resources, time, and effort in the "acquisition of information" prior to a purchase, whereas a passive customer has no desire and finds the experience of little importance. Active customers are valuable sources of information since they communicate with others through word of mouth, extolling the positive or negative attributes of a hospitality enterprise. The frontline employee is the central figure in this exchange of information and the major source of good or bad messages. By managing the communication system and insuring employee satisfaction, vital steps are taken toward more effectively shaping a customer's expectations. As in the tourist and recreation literature, the expectancy model is also linked to understanding customer satisfaction-dissatisfaction.

The Hospitality Expectancy Model

Hotels are organizations of social control for the tourist to "ensure that guests receive individual attention" (Wood, 1994, pp. 65, 77-78). Since the appearance of personalized attention to guests is provided through a collective delivery system, mechanisms of control are used to define expectations, restrict space and interaction, and insure dealing with a relatively select market. In a sense, hotels manage to select clients on the bases of socioeconomic class, and provide privacy by restricting spatial movement. Control over such public-private divisions also reinforces the "expectation of parties to the exchange of hospitality." Decorum, manners, and displays of mutual respect also contribute to guest's expectations of service and help maintain the lines of interaction. Hotels as social institutions "have closely followed home-centered values, as would be expected of organizations that exist to service, as surrogates, the domestic needs of those who are away from their homes." Control strategies grounded in space restriction, privacy, cleanliness, and the expression of other home-centered values must be offered in a subtle manner so as not to detract from the expectation of the "image of freedom." The element of freedom "attached to modern touristic experiences in their (the hotel's) advertising is not easily reconciled with the self-regulation and discipline of the modern hotel." It is an extremely fine service line that is indeed difficult to maintain. However, the illusion for the customer of being the object of attention with detailed service options helps reinforce the self-image of freedom within the privacy of his room.

Besides freedom and privacy, other expectations are sought from the hospitality situation. In an attempt to better explain satisfaction in the service situation, pioneering steps were taken by Getty and Thompson (1994, p. 81), who apply the SERVQUAL model to the lodging industry. "Perceived lodging quality is defined as the consumer's global judgment or attitude relating to the perceived superiority of the lodging service provided by a given property." This definition of lodging quality is consistent with subjective or user-based definitions of service quality. The five attributes of the service quality model SERVQUAL are the starting point for developing a lodging instrument LODGQUAL, which is tailored to meet the needs of each particular situation. Research procedures and data-reduction techniques are tested to determine whether they are effective in developing such a model. Through both data-reduction techniques and subsequent scale identification, the researchers discover that the attributes of tangibility and reliability are clearly differentiated, but that assurance, empathy, and responsiveness merge into a single-scale item encompassing interpersonal exchanges between client and service provider. Again, this confirms the significance of meaningful communication. In developing this technique, Getty and Thompson (1994, pp. 75–96) are most astute in recognizing situational differences, and feel the procedures used to form the scale for this study can also be reproduced for other individual properties. Most importantly, the LODGQUAL scale is found to be positively associated with a series of questions assessing satisfaction with a service-quality experience. Not only is the model useful for measuring a specific situation, but it also has longitudinal applications. Lodging is not the only consumer area found to benefit from the SERVQUAL model. Ruyter and Wetzels, (1997) also modified it to assess retail quality. These researchers think it is important to measure separate service episodes but also to make longitudinal assessments of quality. Separate retailing service aspects were patterned after the performance attributes found in the model. The modification of the items discriminated between two different test situations. It also lent support to a more dynamic notion of service quality in which separate, distinct episodes may be evaluated against a relationship over time to evaluate any changes in quality of service.

Although the above studies are clearly the exception, there is generally not a sufficient body of empirical research in the scientific journals on hospitality satisfaction and service quality. Oh and Jeong (1996, p. 68) maintain that "consumer satisfaction has remained seriously under-researched in the hospitality industry." In particular, widely accepted consumer satisfaction models such as the expectancy-disconfirmation model are not yet "completely introduced into hospitality research." The researchers are critical of the SERVQUAL model because of the conceptual similarity between the way perceived performance and expectations are used to measure service quality and customer satisfaction. Although there is no complete answer to some of these difficulties in the application of these conceptual models, efforts are being made toward resolving some of the confusion. For example, Barsky's research (1992, p. 57) deserves praise for explaining the limitation of the disconfirmation model. He points out that while the "paradigm measures a customer's belief that a product or service exhibits certain attributes, it does not indicate the role those attributes have in determining overall satisfaction." To be complete, the model needs the expectancy-value theory which "assumes that people act on the basis of what they value and what they anticipate will result from their actions." By combining the two models, Barsky (1992, pp. 52-68) demonstrates that a model of customer satisfaction for the hotel industry can in fact be developed. A survey of guests was conducted utilizing the combined model and attempts were made to measure satisfaction based upon the expectations, perceived performance, and value of a hotel's services. The basic assumption of the model is that the value of service and expectations toward a situation "contribute equally to customer satisfaction." Such empirical research goes a long way toward advancing an understanding of customer satisfaction in the hospitality services field.

In following up on this theoretical explanation, Barsky and Labagh (1992, pp. 36-40) report the results of a customer-satisfaction strategy utilizing this model. The measurements included a customer's expectations, perceptions of the service performance, and the importance of the different service attributes with regard to meeting expectations. Hotel guests are asked if their expectations are being met and how important each is to them. Employee attitudes, location, rooms, and price are found to be the most satisfying customer attributes. Least satisfying attributes include the reception areas, auto parking, services, the facilities, and food and beverages. There are distinct differences between business and pleasure travelers, with price, employee attitude, and room preference showing the most variance. The business traveler is most satisfied with larger rooms (and often requests the same room on subsequent visits), being remembered by the employees and staff, and getting a good price. Problems may occur with service, but if the reception area, facilities, and attitudes of the employees are negatively perceived, customers do not return. "By focusing on customer satisfaction and the guest survey, timely and informed decisions" can be made by managers in regards to service.

The conceptual ingredients of perceived value, expectations, and satisfaction are also tested for hotel services by Bojanic (1996, p. 11). Higher levels of perceived value or what is received result in purchase and repurchase and in higher levels of customer satisfaction. The model used to test the relationship is called "script theory," which is another name for expectancy theory. Like the script for a play, the customer has certain expectations about the kind of service he should expect in a hotel or restaurant based upon past experience. In reviewing other studies that adopted the SERVQUAL model, Bojanic (1996, p. 13) reports that customer expectations increase as hotel prices increase, and that perceived value is a result of a price/quality trade-off affecting satisfaction. "A strong, positive correlation between perceived value and customer satisfaction" supports the theory "that when consumers perceive that they obtained a good value, the firm met or exceeded their expectations and the consumer had a satisfying service experience." The results hold for luxury, high-priced, moderately priced, and budget hotels. The recommendation for service providers is very simple but so important to understand. "Hotels at all levels need to manage value perceptions by understanding how consumers formulate their price and quality perceptions." In particular, hotels need to determine which cues guide consumers to form impressions of quality so that they can close the gap between objective quality and perceived quality. In addition, since price has an effect on "consumer expectations," hotels can also actively manage expectations through advertising and customer socialization by communicating the quality of a service. Just as the disconfirmation theory is not complete without the value-expectancy idea molded into the satisfaction model, so too, the SERVQUAL model may also benefit from the customer's assessment of value associated with service attributes, especially when customer satisfaction is at issue.

The importance or value of customer attributes needs to be uncovered so that the performance perception of a service and whether it is judged desirable or adequate can be weighed to determine satisfaction. In a review of guest surveys, Lewis and Pizam (1981, p. 39) conclude that the survey forms "fail to answer the single-most important question overall, is the guest satisfied or dissatisfied (and will the guest return)? This is the bottom line in assessing guest satisfaction and affects the interpretation of all other data gathered with a survey." In an attempt to establish a survey that discriminates on the basis of satisfaction dissatisfaction, an original list of 41 attributes is reduced through factor analysis to 11 distinct service attributes. These include (1) room and bathroom quality, (2) room and bathroom cleanliness, (3) front-desk services, (4) both relative and actual price, (5) restaurant availability and quality of service, (6) professionalism of the staff, (7) convenience and availability of services, (8) room service, (9) prestige and aesthetic appeal of the property, (10) sports facilities, and (11) bathroom condition and maintenance. In comparing the number-one factor, room and bathroom quality, with the number-eight ranked, room service, there is a 27% difference in the level of importance for determining satisfaction between the attributes. The value associated with an expectation by a customer puts the perception of a performance of service in perspective. A guest may expect room service that is deemed highly desirable and performed at a high level of competence but if it is not highly valued by the customer, the meaning of satisfaction relative to other attributes changes. The remaining examples that stress the importance of attribute values are taken from the few studies done on customer satisfaction within the restaurant industry. Like the need for accommodations, food is also a necessity of extended travel.

A service matrix of attributes forms the basis for making evaluative judgments about what services contribute or detract from a satisfactory experience (Almanza, Jaffe, and Lin, 1994). A gap model that looks at "customer satisfaction is a result of what customers think will happen (expectations), interacting with what customers think did happen (perceptions)." A matrix of service attributes are used to "rank the importance of these attributes so that resources may be directed to those that are most important to customers" (Almanza et al., 1994, pp. 64, 67). A university cafeteria provides a setting for the study; however, this implies that expectations within a tourist setting are almost likely to be quite different. As in a deviant case analysis, and since there are so few studies in the area, the findings are likely to provide a contrast to a tourist situation. In general, the most important attributes to the customers in the university cafeteria are quality of food, convenient location, cleanliness, and reasonable price. These are all ranked in the top five in importance across all meal periods. The least important attributes are availability of takeout, decor, a meeting place, availability of coffee and drink refills, and atmosphere. These attributes are all ranked among the bottom five in importance for all meals. Although it is mere speculation, foodservice attributes in a tourist situation are likely to be reversed in their rank order of importance. This cafeteria study provides a benchmark for future comparison.

In a non-tourist foodservice study sampling fast food establishments, the findings suggest "that customers' expectations could be effective criteria for segmenting the fast-food market" for purposes of measuring satisfaction (Oh and Jeong, 1996, pp. 74-80). On the basis of 19 attributes measuring customers' levels of expectations, distinct market segments could be identified. They are identified by a customer type. There is the "neat service seeker" who highly ranks the tangible appearance of the physical plant (cleanliness and neatness) and the responsiveness of the service (employee attitude and greetings). The "classic diner" is more interested in the atmosphere, food quality, and service response while the "convenience seeker" expects quick service plus a product in an appropriate setting. And finally, the "indifferent diner" cares little about the products or services of a fast food restaurant. How well the restaurants performed in delivering these expectations affects the customers' perceived satisfaction of the situation. Thirty-seven percent of the explained variance for all the types of fast food customers' perceptions are related to the tangible attributes of the restaurant (cleanliness, neatness, spaciousness, location), the responsiveness of the employees (quick food delivery, employee attitude), and reliability of the food product (tastiness, price, and quality). Given the types of customers identified by expectations, this study also provides a basis for segmenting customers across more traditional social demographic lines. However, marketers are strongly encouraged "to pursue market segmentation strategies based on behavioral variables such as expectations, rather than conventional social demographic variables that could provide only simple descriptions of the market" (Oh and Jeong, 1996, p. 81). Not only are attributes identified but also these are associated with a specific type of diner that takes the analysis one step further toward a better understanding of a clientele role.

> Employee attitudes, location, rooms, and price are found to be the most satisfying customer attributes.

The significance of attributes also dominates other studies by Ladki and Nomani (1996, pp. 28-30) who observe that "existing studies in food service offer little or no interest in understanding consumer involvement in product or service to determine satisfaction." The sample of restaurant consumers of ethnic cuisine is from the Washington, D.C., area and restaurant attributes are used to determine consumer satisfaction. The most frequently mentioned attributes indicated for ensuring customer satisfaction include "(1) speed of service, (2) restaurant hours of operation, food eye appeal, and restaurant reputation, (3) the recommendation of a friend, availability of nutritional information, appropriate selection of regional ethnic dishes, personnel competency in food production/sanitation, and employee's courtesy." While many of the same attributes are shared in the studies mentioned above, the situational context and style of restaurants seem to be a determining factor in how patrons respond to the service attributes.

Because "service" may be a common denominator across many different kinds of situations, some researchers attempt to apply the SERVQUAL model in assessing customer perceptions of service quality in restaurants (Bojanic and Rosen, 1994). The researchers examine a chain restaurant with a sophisticated saloon, catering to a wide variety of clientele (families, students, and couples). The attributes most significant in assessing service quality are "knowing the customer, reliability, and assurance." The major difference with this model and the standard SERVQUAL model is that the empathy attribute is segmented into two dimensions, knowing the customer and being given access. The largest gaps between expectations and perceptions are associated with reliability and responsiveness, the smallest gap for knowing the customer. "Customers of the restaurant feel it is important to experience some degree of personalized attention" even though their expectations are rather low in this area. The restaurant in this study fared well because the quality gap (perception-expectations) is the lowest for "knowing the customer." This turned out to be the most important dimension of overall quality. That is precisely why it is necessary to perform a complete review when shortfalls begin to rise. Improvements in reliability can be made through "changes in operations," while changes in assurance may need to be improved through "internal marketing and training" (Bojanic and Rosen, 1994, p. 9).

In a final example of restaurant service quality and satisfaction by Dube, Renaghan, and Miller (1994, pp. 41-45), a set of 35 attributes is reduced to the most salient by applying factor-analytic techniques and selecting the highest rated item in each factor. Paralleling the SERVQUAL or RATER model, seven of the most significant attributes are selected. Three relate to the tangible attribute and four relate to reliability, assurance, responsiveness, and empathy. The next step is developing scenarios that combine each of the seven attributes but vary two attributes in each scenario. In one instance you vary the attribute positively and in another negatively. For example, you are seated as soon as you arrive (positive expectation) or you wait 15 minutes (negative expectation). The authors apply a form of conjoint analysis that simultaneously measures all seven attributes each time, but varies the extremes of some attributes each time. The logic behind this approach assumes respondents do not have to evaluate the importance of each attribute, one at a time, while unrealistically imagining that all the others are kept constant. This approach does include some redundancy, limits the number of attributes that can be tested, and overlooks the independence of the attributes that distinguish them from each other in a customer's mental judgment. Despite the advantages and disadvantages of such an approach, some interesting comparisons between business and pleasure diners arise regarding those attributes affecting satisfaction. "Although business and pleasure respondents both placed the greatest importance on food taste, and the second greatest on attentive service, there the similarities ended" (Dube at al., 1994, pp. 41-45). Pleasure diners are less sensitive to time spent waiting on a table but care about menu variety, while the opposite is true for the business diner. If improvements are to be made in service, food quality, taste, and staff attentiveness are the most sensitive areas to consider. Despite the small number of empirical studies, a recent awakening seems to promise more concrete data in the future.

CONCLUSION

If you combine an asset approach to tourism that seeks to identify value among the travel elements with a systems approach that identifies the organizational elements that are interrelated to fulfil a travel experience, you come away with a framework that forces the researcher to identity those processes that create a dynamic experience. A process that is most critical to a tourist experience is acquiring satisfaction in each phase of the travel process. There are three major organizational units and roles that are essential for a tourist experience to take place. The tourist role provides the key ingredient concerning what is expected. The tourist is also linked to recreational expectations and hospitality considerations about accommodations and restaurants that are intertwined into the total experience.

Tourism, leisure-recreation, and hospitality are united into a system that offers positive reinforcement such as fun, pleasure, rest, enjoyment, and excitement to increase personal satisfaction. This is not just some kind of frivolous secondary or tertiary consideration in the affairs of humankind but apparently a central life concern that effects life satisfaction. Having tourist experiences throughout a person's life helps to create a positive outlook toward life and buoy the spirits. Persons may face difficult and rigorous challenges in their lives but travel provides a legitimate outlet from these pressures. The few satisfaction studies that measure the effects of travel demonstrate positive results for recreational travelers.

Knowledge of customer expectations in travel, leisure-recreation, and hospitality is essential to understanding how satisfaction is determined. The perception of a service performance in a travel situation, and how important or valued it is by the customer, is also part of the equation affecting customer satisfaction. Combined in a reliable marketing survey, evaluation of a traveler's expectations, perceptions of performance, and the value of attributes are key factors in explaining satisfaction. It is especially important that those programs, facilities, and services most amenable to change be evaluated through some kind of empirical quantitative process so that customer judgments can be assessed. In the next chapter, a series of quantitative case studies are reviewed in an attempt to identify those specifying attributes in a tourist situation that affect satisfaction.

*The problem of specification in measurement is essential
to understanding an attitude of satisfaction.*

■ 4

Attribute Indicators and Specifying Satisfaction

WHY ATTRIBUTES AND SPECIFICATION?

The Problem of Identifying Indicators

THE LITERATURE on leisure, recreation, tourism, and marketing offers up some empirical cues to help understand and define situational behavioral action affecting satisfaction. Making sense of the numerous behavioral responses involved with a day trip, an overnight, a holiday, or a vacation is a challenge. Identifying specific kinds of indicators of satisfaction among those responses that are part of the daily operations of an organization is an elementary first step toward understanding what potentially increases or decreases satisfaction, or conversely increases or decreases dissatisfaction in a situation. For the most part, this chapter compares the results of surveys previously gathered from tourists visiting national parks to explore how attributes in a tourist situation are specified.

This research work on satisfaction began in the 1980s and is still evolving, along with the scales and measurement approach. Though still incomplete, much progress has been made through the efforts of university professionals with the cooperation of National Park Service personnel. A chronological presentation of issues, as dealt with in the surveys, provides an overview of this work. Two issues dominate the research: namely, identifying indicators or attributes of satisfaction and specifying a satisfaction model. Details of the surveys are being kept to a minimum, since much about the methods, field techniques, statistics, and data tables are available in cited reports or published articles. The goal is simply to report the findings and implications as they relate to satisfaction. But before discussing the results of these surveys, a brief introduction to the problem and conceptual model that guided this research is necessary to facilitate a better understanding.

In the process of conducting these surveys, it became evident that the practical usefulness of the findings is greater when data pertain to specific program components, rather than complex global programs or general issues (Rutman, 1977). In fact, Mandell (1989, pp. 174-200) argues that understanding different settings is critical for assessing how programs and policies vary in effectiveness. Social situations are hardly identical, but there are organizational attributes that fulfil basic functions or serve common expectations in providing satisfactory experiences. How that process unfolds is the subject of investigation.

The problem of specification in measurement is essential to understanding an attitude of satisfaction. Identifying the precise content of an attitude with a criterion variable is a strategy advocated by Fishbein and Ajzen (1975) as a remedy for the low correlation between verbal expressions and how respondents act. Avoiding a mismatch between abstract statements and very specific criteria is judged to be a strategy for improving attitude predictions. A study by Heberlein and Black (1976) examines the effects of attitudinal "specificity" and finds that higher correlation resulted when scales are more specific. The findings offer "evidence for the hypothesis that attitude measures that are more specific to a given behavior are better predictors of that behavior than are more general measures" (Heberlein and Black, 1976, p. 478). But that finding is not universally supported by subsequent studies. For Fischer and Farina (1978, p. 597), the specificity of attitude has little impact, since attitude scales consist of abstract belief statements.

Despite the abstractness of a scale, individuals form definite opinions and take corresponding actions. Such opposite findings are also reported by Kahle, Klingel, and Kulka (1981), who find that despite the relative abstractness of an attitude like "outgoingness," comparability between the behavioral items and attitude is achieved resulting in discriminate construct validity. Such a successful finding is attributed to assuring "comparability of attitudes and behavior items," although the attitudinal construct was most general and abstract. Since opinion varies on defining attitudinal indicators, the ability to determine effective levels of abstractness and specification of an attitude scale appears to be a confusing issue in operationalizing measures. Given the rather inconclusive evidence for either position, it is essential to continue testing the relationship between abstract and specific scales in research designs.

The measurement model adopted in the national park surveys assumes a more direct approach for determining satisfaction. The current model is specified in such a way that the scale items ask the respondents to make a series of judgments about their experiences in terms of satisfaction. The actions or behaviors are broken down first into component parts. Specific services, facilities, and programs are identified that facilitate achieving a pleasurable end. Functionalists historically emphasize actions to obtain specific ends that are more rationally defined. These are called *instrumental actions*. A much broader usage is taken in the cases reported and includes detailed components of a leisure-tourist situation such as transportation and communication services, facilities providing rest, relief, and refreshment, and provider roles offering direction and information. A practical rule used to guide selection of attributes is whether they are subject to managerial control through modification and change. This may not be the best rule but certainly is appealing to managers and decision makers who are responsible for providing public service. The emphasis is on the more specific components of a social situation.

Satisfaction is not only influenced by the above specific attributes, but also by less concrete possibilities. Borrowing again from the functionalists, the term *expressive action* refers to the internal states of respondents designating more subjective, emotional responses. Csikszentmahalyi (1981, pp. 135-138) comes closest to identifying leisure as expressive activity that provides immediate "intrinsic rewards as opposed to delayed gratification." In the strictest sense, expressiveness could be interpreted as the behavioral product of some subjective, inner-emotional state. Iso-Ahola (1980, p. 231) also stressed the importance of intrinsic rewards that are built into the activity, such as "gratification in winning or losing a game, pursuit of happiness, and self-actualization." Emphasis is directed to the psychological or subjective state as the respondents in the surveys interpret them. Expectations or actions defining the central purpose of the activity such as touring an historic fort, fishing, visiting a beach, or participating in a river-floating event are actions that are meant to gratify the tourist or participant with positive reinforcement. In specifying scale attributes, the concepts of instrumental and expressive are adapted to a leisure situation such as touring a national park or seeking out activities that are available at these sites. The above ideas are abstracted, paraphrased, and taken directly from the first case study that began our interest in trying to better predict and understand satisfaction of park tourists and visitors (Noe, 1987). That study set the tone for the rest of the surveys that follow.

Instrumental and Expressive Attributes

Instrumental attributes are means used by the tourist to achieve some desired end, while the *expressive attributes* are the psychological or social benefits derived by participating in a recreational goal such as fishing, swimming, sightseeing, taking a boat tour, etc. In reviewing recreation-leisure studies, either expressive or instrumental attributes are commonly part of the attempts at measuring participant satisfaction. The labeling of the attributes as either expressive or instrumental, together or separately, is not a theoretical distinction explicitly recognized, but implicitly utilized by some researchers in widely different leisure, recreation, and travel situations. In a study by Kelly, Langenau, and Levine (1990), for example, seven dimensions of turkey hunting are identified. Facilitating an activity, the instrumental behavior is judged differently from the harvest or the expressive, more goal-oriented behavior. In this case, the instrumental process of lo-

> **S**atisfaction is not only influenced by the above specific attributes but also by less concrete possibilities.

cating and calling turkeys is evaluated differently than the satisfaction derived from the harvest, the expressive culmination of the activity.

Recreational visitor satisfaction is also measured with respect to facility design and maintenance. In developing a model of visitor satisfaction for a walking trail within a Chicago preserve, the instrumental attributes of the trail, including surface, length, terrain, and proximity to residence contributed less to visitor satisfaction than the changes in visual perspective and preference. The visual and emotionally positive experience of sightseeing is more important than the properties of the trail that afforded the experience (Lieber and Fesenmaier, 1985). In another case, the emphasis shifts for a travel and tourist study that finds a mix between instrumental and expressive attributes affecting levels of satisfaction. Two instrumental service features, including a guided tour service and the location at the point of departure, along with the more expressive attribute of sightseeing, are singled out as significantly contributing to the satisfaction of the trip (Whipple and Thach, 1988).

Still another tourist-recreational study measures camper satisfaction in the Adirondack Mountains. Three attributes are identified as being critical. The expressive camping attribute resulted in feelings of solitude/rejuvenation and nature appreciation. The instrumental characteristic, pertaining to facility conditions, is also cited as a factor. The most critical overall, however, is experiencing solitude and rejuvenation, while the importance of other attributes varied by site (Connelly, 1987). For the most part, both the expressive and instrumental attributes in these studies are measured to determine satisfaction with the recreational experience. The attributes varied in significance as contributors to satisfaction.

Some satisfaction studies are more limiting in the extent of analysis and stress only the expressive dimension of behavior. A study by Lounsbury and Polik (1992) evaluates four expressive-related needs adopted from Beard and Ragheb's leisure-motivation scale relating to vacation behavior. The intellectual, social, competence-mastery, and stimulus-avoidance attributes are measured in relationship to reported satisfaction. All four expressive attributes are positively related to satisfaction. In such cases, expressive attributes are commonly compared and evaluated with respect to each other. For example, the reported satisfaction of residents adjacent to Moore Park in Metro Toronto is based more on visual appreciation rather than recreational use (Bornstein, Milliken, and Fitzgibbon, 1985). A sense of refuge symbolized in the visual experience of the landscape typography offers greater expressive satisfaction than the recreational opportunities.

Research studies also emphasize instrumental attributes, such as dealing with facility restrooms, fencing, lighting, shade, or building conditions (Bartlett and Einert, 1992). These studies usually assess the facilities and services that management directly controls. Such a study by Vaske, Donnelly, and Williamson (1991) monitors the quality of service in New Hampshire state parks by stressing the instrumental dimension of satisfaction. Instrumental behavior is not only important for understanding physical and contextual environmental conditions, but it also helps us understand how role interactions between the service worker and the customer, or between customers, are managed in the tourist situation. Successful management of those interactions in the service situation is "crucial" for maximizing "customer satisfaction" (Mahoney, 1987).

Instrumental and expressive attributes in the above recreation and tourist studies are distinguished as defining a range of attributes in a situation. In marketing research, the interpretation of instrumental and expressive is very similar. Swan and Combs (1976) define *instrumental performance* as the means to an end or the evaluation of a physical product, while the *expressive attribute* is the personal experience of the end in itself or the psychological interpretation of a product. Given this perspective, they assert that satisfaction is produced only through the expressive experience.

In social action theory, both concepts are treated as necessary for human action. Both are goal directed with the instrumental being more cognitively oriented, whereas the expressive is more emotional or feeling oriented. The evaluative mode of behavior is more associated with expressive acts within the context of social action theory. In essence, Czepiel and Rosenberg (1977) consider these as factors which "truly motivate and contribute to satisfaction," while the instrumental are maintenance attributes which, if absent, create dissatisfaction. In our testing of the expressive-instrumental model, given the fact that so few studies have tested this attribute model, it is reasonable to speculate that instrumental attributes also influence satisfaction along with the expressive.

ATTRIBUTE ANALYSIS OF SELECT NATIONAL PARK VISITORS

First Stage of Testing Attribute Model—Evaluations and Problems

Managers of natural areas such as national parks are becoming more sensitive to site-specific information about the park visitor and tourist. At the same time, the type of information being sought is shifting from descriptive to more explanatory. Instead of being content with trip information on destinations, user demographics, and levels of public use of a park, today's managers are seeking to understand attributes that affect public reactions. In an address to participants attending a social science short course at Virginia Polytechnic Institute and State University in 1992, Gary Everhardt, former director of the National Park Service, recognizes a need to be more aware of "public expectations and how to better accommodate them without destroying the very thing they come to experience—the nature of the park." If national park staffs are going to be more responsive to perceived problems, judgments, and evaluations of the tourist public, then it is necessary for parks to monitor public responses to park experiences. Cutting-edge data that ask direct and pointed questions of the public about their evaluation of a park's management of services are required.

Managers of public, outdoor recreation areas need confirmation from the tourist that the facilities, services, and programs provided are generally satisfactory. Measuring quality and service is premised on what Manning (1985, p. 6) refers to as "evaluative communication between visitors and managers." Developing effective ways of soliciting accurate and reliable feedback from the public about an outdoor recreational experience presents certain measurement problems, one of which is properly limiting the definition of an outdoor recreational situation. As part of the proposed solution to that problem, the following research projects attempt to sharpen scaling techniques by testing whether instrumental and expressive attributes are distinct behavioral indicators that are effective predictors of satisfaction.

Expressive indicators involve core experiences representing the major intent of an act, in this case seeking a satisfactory outdoor experience in a park (swimming, sightseeing, camping, hiking a nature trail, touring a fort, floating a river, etc.), while instrumental indicators serve to act as facilitators toward achieving that desired end (parking, rental services, restrooms, concession services, etc.). These distinctions are used to specifically define characteristics of a park situation that possibly affect satisfaction. The tourist judgment of satisfaction is also possibly affected by past exposure or unfulfilled expectations. The importance of specifying the attributes of a park situation through an evaluative process hopes to provide a greater understanding of what affects satisfaction. A number of parks served as sites to test the initial model and various modifications of it.

The results of the national park visitor surveys include data synthesized from the following parks: the Chattahoochee National Recreation Area, the Blue Ridge Parkway, Gulf Islands National Seashore, Castillo de San Marcos National Monument, Biscayne National Park, Cape Lookout National Seashore, Moores Creek National Battlefield, and the U.S. Virgin Islands National Park-St. John. The studies span the 1980s to the mid-1990s. A seasonally adjusted survey is used in most cases except for the Chattahoochee River rafting festival, where participants are contacted on the day of the event. A cluster-sampling technique is used in randomly contacting park users during the a.m. and p.m. hours to determine a willingness to participate in the study. A single week is selected for the spring, summer, and fall. An attempt to sample the Blue Ridge in the winter failed because of the weather and too few visitors to justify the expense.

At Castillo de San Marcos, winter visitors are included in the survey since this is the only park surveyed whose public-use figures pointed to four distinct seasons of use. In randomly selecting a week for each season, only those weeks without holidays, festivals, or local community promotions are selected to optimize sampling a general park user and not some specialized user. The park visitors are intercepted at entrance points following a random process, and if agreeable, they would receive a mail questionnaire. A modified Dillman approach is utilized to insure adequate return rates. Acceptable response rates range from a low of 50% for the Chattahoochee River rafting event to a high of 76.7% for the Blue Ridge Parkway. Findings are presented in roughly the same chronological order in which the studies took place, beginning with the Chattahoochee River rafting event.

Case Studies
The Chattahoochee National Recreation Area

In 1978, Congress authorized the establishment of a 48-mile national recreation area between Atlanta and Buford Dam. The river begins as a spring-fed stream in the north Georgia mountains and flows south across the state of Georgia to the Gulf of Mexico. A river event provided the opportunity to test if understanding instrumental qualities increased the predictability of satisfaction as opposed to obtaining an assessment based solely on expressive qualities.

Public services including law enforcement, safety, parking, transportation, and communication are instrumental activities that are adaptable to change. While it is true that distinct instrumental activities factor into distinct activities, they contributed little to the explained variance of overall satisfaction. For this study, increased specification of attributes did not result in increased predictability. Event festivities such as the partying, music, and revelry among the rafters account for most of the explained satisfaction. Since the expressive activity is the major function of the event, it is not surprising that it dominates the satisfaction of the participants (Noe, 1987). High satisfaction is found only among the five expressive attributes. Of the 24 attributes, highest dissatisfaction is found among the instrumental attributes with restroom facilities, parking availability, traffic to and from the event, and food and beverage facilities leading the list. Those attending the event are generally satisfied with the overall organization at 65%, while 13.8% are dissatisfied, and the remaining are neutral or uncommitted (Aveni, 1980). The concepts of instrumental and expressive attributes differentiated between activities within the context of this organized event. Data leading to these results are found in the report by Aveni (1980).

The Blue Ridge Parkway

This roadway transverses the states of Virginia and North Carolina along a 470-mile-long corridor through the crest of the southern Appalachians. The parkway is noted for its scenic beauty, historical sites of a past agrarian way of life, and outdoor recreation. In effect, it links Shenandoah National Park in the north to the Great Smoky Mountains National Park to the south.

In evaluating the adequacy of the facilities, services, and programs along the parkway, a number of attributes stand out. The most satisfying are the expressive character of the parkway represented by an enjoyable driving and riding experience; a road opening up nature's beauty; a clean, litter-free road; a road adequately restricting commercial development; a road providing a quiet, visual experience; and a road with nicely designed guard rails, shoulders, bridges, and tunnels. The least satisfying attributes are found among the instrumental characteristics. Services such as providing reasonable auto repair and fuel, emergency communication facilities, adequate directional signs, and sufficient camping facilities are attributes that cause some parkway visitors about 10% dissatisfaction.

In trying to uncover specific problems with an experience, a list of potential problems was constructed in consultation with park rangers from typical types of complaints received from tourists in the past. Despite the 20 items thought to cause problems, only a few tourists indicated they encountered any such problem. Interestingly, some problems such as "not enough wildlife and too many insects" are completely out of the control of managers, while other situations can be effectively managed by providing "enough signs giving information and directions, or offering enough information on the history or the natural environment."

In evaluating the Virginia northern section of the parkway, only fishing at Peaks of Otter and the James River received a less than good rating. For the southern North Carolina section of the parkway, overall evaluations are positive except for the concession services at Crabtree Meadows. Negative evaluations still represent few tourists. Despite being a small part of the tourist body, those disgruntled tourists tell others of their dissatisfaction. Yet the grocery store, restaurant, gift shop, and restrooms can be upgraded since this is under direct management control. Although fishing conditions are determined by natural forces, optimum times can be predicted and posted to maximize a tourist's chances of success in an otherwise chance situation. The majority of parkway users are more interested in sightseeing, walking for pleasure, picnicking, outdoor photography, nature walks, and visiting fairs, activities more comparable with the core purpose of the parkway. Data leading to these results is found in the report by the Center for Public and Urban Research, G.S.U. (1987).

Second Stage of Testing the Attribute Model—Expectations Added to Model

In addition to evaluation and problem attributes, park studies in the southeast region began to incorporate information on expectations. It became evident that a measure of tourist satisfaction is a multidimensional concept including not just an evaluational dimension but other variables that affect satisfaction ratings. The expectations of a customer have proved to be one such dimension. Perceived disconfirmation theory, included in the marketing literature as a type of contrast theory, describes the discrepancy between actual participation and expectations as perceived by the user. It is usually measured with a question that asks how closely the product or service approaches that which the respondent expected. This dimension of satisfaction is included in a number of studies, including Westbrook (1980), Oliver and Oliver (1981), Swan and Trawick (1981), Westbrook and Oliver (1981), Bearden and Teel (1983), Westbrook and Reilly (1983), and Tse and Wilton (1988).

If the more recent marketing literature is used to describe perceived disconfirmation, "consumers would compare perceived performance to the recalled expectations which may not match pre-consumption expectations because of cognitive dissonance, assimilation, or contrast" (Yi, 1990). In all probability, previous use and expectations are modified by the actual experience, and differ from the initial impressions in part because of dissonance reduction and assimilation. In order to avoid this confounding situation, future studies will measure the perceptions of a service first, followed by the expectations of the customer toward that service. This is a format also recommended by Schneider and Bowen (1995, p. 35) who assert that asking customers what they realistically expect will produce more "reality-oriented responses." In measuring expectations, respondents are asked whether they expected more or fewer services, facilities, or programs.

Balance or cognitive consistency theory may also play a role in satisfaction explanations in that differences in the use of a site by a person may function to reduce dissonance and modify expectations. Infrequent travel or limited site use by a tourist may leave expectations unchanged because of the limited experience, as opposed to a tourist who frequents a site and may stay for longer periods. For the most part, the studies that are part of this second stage of the model added the expectation variable, and one study tested the past use variable. It is already evident that the satisfaction model is still incomplete, and will need to include other variables in the future. But for now, a brief review of these completed surveys is provided to give some idea of how this research has proceeded up to this time.

Case Studies
Biscayne National Park

The park is centered on Biscayne Bay and is a water-based natural recreation area. At the north end, the park is bordered by Key Biscayne, Chicken Key, and Bill Braggs Cape State Park. The south border is Key Largo, John Pennekamp Coral Reef State Park, and Key Largo Coral Reef Marine Sanctuary. On the west side, the park is bordered by the state of Florida and Biscayne Bay itself, while on the east a string of keys runs from the

> Expressive expectations of attributes dominate satisfaction responses.

north to the south. There are major facilities and services located at Boca Chita, Elliot, and Adams Key, and beyond the keys is a line of reefs running north to south that provides mooring, anchorage, and navigational aids.

In evaluating the park experience, the vast majority of the boating public agreed that the park offers a safe place for boating, provides access to the water and outdoor recreation opportunities, and offers a quiet visual experience along with an enjoyable diving experience. The expressive attributes again emerge as dominant factors influencing satisfaction. On the negative side, instrumental factors again appear to have more of an effect on perceptions of dissatisfaction. Insufficient docking, lack of convenient restrooms, directional signs and navigational aids, inadequate shower facilities, and crowding stood out as concerns for a minority of the tourists. Those experiencing problems are concerned with poor fishing, crowding, litter, dirty restrooms and showers, too many insects, bay pollution, and reckless boat operators. But some boaters do not perceive such problems.

The differences in perceptions seem, in part, to be a result of environmental attitudes; some tourists favor a more developed park as opposed to those tourists who want a more natural experience (Jurowski, Uysal, Williams, and Noe, 1995). Expectations tend to support more management intervention to provide more ranger patrols, more aggressive enforcement of safety rules, more regulation on boaters around diving areas, more designated diving and wildlife-viewing areas, more anchorage and mooring areas, more picnic areas, clean toilets, parking facilities, mosquito control in camping areas, navigational aids, and less commercial fishing. There is a consistency in the responses that helps focus management attention on those key problems perceived by the park tourist. Data leading to these results are found in a report by Snow (1989).

Castillo de San Marcos National Monument

This historic park is located in St. Augustine, Florida, in an historic district and includes two forts, Castillo de San Marcos and Matanzas. The original fortifications date back to the first Spanish influence in North America, then the English, and finally to their use by the United States in the early part of the last century as points of defense along the eastern seaboard. The ratings of the touring public are consistently high across all the four seasons of the park. The expressive attributes associated with the ranger staff, including their presentations, demonstrations, and interpretive programs at Castillo de San Marcos, are ranked as being excellent. The friendly, polite staff is further rated highly because of their informal discussions with the public and the quality of their formal presentations describing the history of the fort.

The next highly rated set of attributes is also expressive in nature and highlights the appearance of the fort. The tourist liked the appearance of the lawn and grassy surfaces, the trees and shrubs, the flowers, the cannon deck, the cannon firings, and the absence of litter. Conversely, the attributes that are least appreciated encompass instrumental factors that repeatedly appear in all four seasons of the year among different samples. The availability of parking, benches for resting, and audio boxes are three instrumental attributes receiving poor ratings. However, an expressive attribute dealing with the appearance of the moat (an area easily despoiled by floating litter and the stagnant appearance of the shallow water) also received a poor rating. This is one of the few times in these studies of various national park situations that an expressive attribute received negative ratings.

Similar results from the seasonal surveys at Fort Matanzas again demonstrate the importance of highly received, expressive attributes such as the appearance of the grounds, as well as the interpretive talk on the ferry ride to the fort. The availability of parking and information received poor ratings as instrumental factors, following the same pattern as other park studies.

Expectations of the tourist public revolve around the forts and their structures that are so unique from a 20th-century perspective. The tourists fully expect to be informed about the history of the forts and how the people lived in them. They want to see displays of historic artifacts and costumes. The tourists also expect the fort's personnel to be knowledgeable and available to answer questions, or they expect audio presentations on the fort's history. Finally, the tourists expect a place to park and places to sit and rest. Many of these latter items are lacking at the forts, and such instrumental issues are not uncommon in park operations. There also are a number of attributes that are clearly not expected, such as video presentations; a museum with light, sound, and visually animated displays; a shop to get snacks and drinks; or a picnic area inside the fort. Live reenactments of period life and cannon firings, although not expected, received favorable ratings. Obviously, other attributes associated with the forts are held in higher regard.

Parking tops the list of problems associated with the forts. Castillo de San Marcos is located in a historic district in downtown St. Augustine. Space is not available nor would a parking deck be in keeping with the historic district and Spanish Quarter adjacent to the fort. Shuttle transportation, while not as convenient as curbside parking, is viable if the limiting conditions of the situation are explained properly. This study also highlights expressive attributes and finds again that some instrumental attributes are found lacking. Data leading to these findings are in a report by the Survey Research Center, G.S.U. (1990a).

Virgin Islands National Park at St. John, U.S.V.I.

This study was undertaken on St. John in the Caribbean, West Indies. A little over half of St. John became a national park in 1956, when Laurence S. Rockefeller and a Jackson Hole, Wyoming, preservation group donated the land to the federal government for the protection of marine resources. It covers approximately 20 square miles; 56% of the park is land based while the remaining is under water and laced with coral reefs. One of the 10 most beautiful beaches in the world is located at Trunk Bay, with other beach sites scattered around the island. The park offers outdoor recreation activities such as camping, hiking, and nature walks, and of course water-based activities such as snorkeling, swimming, and boating. There are also a number of privately owned, full-service resorts catering to the tourist, and the Virgin Islands are a free port offering duty-free purchases.

In evaluating the facilities of the visitor center at Cruz Bay, for example, the expressive functions of the center such as the informational displays and the informal staff interaction with the tourist received high marks. The tangible aspects, such as being litter free and the landscaping, are also valued. The instrumental attributes such as clean, odor-free restrooms, drinking water and refreshments, availability of seating for resting, and directional signs are poorly rated. At Hawksnest and Trunk Bays, the highest rating held up the beaches, the swimming and wading, the clean and sandy beach areas, the snorkeling, and helpfulness of the lifeguards. Again, the tourists poorly rated the instrumental attributes such as directional and information signs, the restrooms and their cleanliness, changing areas, and showers. Since the survey, the restrooms, showers, and changing areas at Trunk Bay have received major upgrading and changes.

At Cinnamon Bay, the beach, swimming area, and covered picnic area are rated highly as expressive attributes. The small site museum received the poorest rating as an expressive attribute, while restrooms, as an instrumental factor, also received a poor rating. However, the poor rating represents only a small minority of the tourists at this site. Most of the instrumental services, such as food and shopping options, are provided by a concession operation that is perceived as offering good to excellent service. In evaluating the responses of the tourists to what are perceived as problems affecting the sites on St. John, only a few attributes are singled out for criticism. Dirty restrooms, lack of privacy in restrooms and changing areas, and inadequate beach changing areas are cited by the tourists as being problematic.

In measuring expectations among tourists to St. John, Jurowski Uysal, and Noe (1993, p. 13) find differences in the environmental attitudes among tourists that affect what they expect. The more consumptive tourist types seem to expect and value an increase in signage, beach shelters, more pull-offs along the road to view scenery, information, picnic areas, toilet facilities with more supplies, hiking trails, guided tours, and more historic ruins to visit. The more conservation type of tourist appears to expect and want less-visible man-made structures, fewer people on the beaches, and more wildlife and vegetation projects. This group also places some value on guided tours and hiking trails but not to the extent that the more consumptive tourist expects.

Not only do these expectations parallel what is valued in expressive and instrumental attributes and perceptions of problems, but also they seem to be related to differences in environmental attitudes. For the more commercially oriented tourist services, consumptive attitudes toward travel services might be equally important for differentiating among customers. Data for the St. John sites at the national park in the Virgin Islands are taken from a report by the Survey Research Center, G.S.U. (1990b).

Moores Creek National Battlefield

The site commemorates one of the earliest patriot victories of the American Revolutionary War. On February 27, 1776, a battle between British loyalists and American patriots took place at a site approximately 20 miles northwest of present day Wilmington, NC. After the American victory, the strength of the patriot cause grew throughout the Carolinas, discouraging loyalist involvement in the South. The visitor center contains a museum with displays of period clothing, a weapons exhibit, a slide presentation explaining the battle, and a gift shop. Trails permit tourists and visitors to view the sites of the battle and at various points the interpretative displays, audio stations, and monuments help explain and represent what happened that day. The park also provides a picnic area with shelters and a special-event center for use by the local community. Seven out of 10 of the day visitors are residents of North Carolina.

Unexpectedly, an instrumental attribute of adequate parking is found to be the top-ranked factor in assessing the battlefield and visitor center. This is unusual given the dominance of expressive attributes. However, the remaining top-rated attributes are expressive and include a friendly and available staff for questions, absence of litter, the appearance of the grounds and monuments, as well as the reconstructed bridge and history trail, the historical information, and the discussions, explanations, and demonstration programs. The ratings of the top-rated attributes are in the 90% level.

The attributes evaluated poorly included the availability of benches for resting, not unlike the finding at Castillo de San Marcos. Other instrumental attributes rated on the poor to fair side are informational and directional signage. Two of the poorly to fairly rated attributes included expressive attributes referring to the size and number of displays in the park museum. In reviewing the perception of problems listed by the tourists, directional and informational signage and not enough information, the small size of the visitor center housing the museum, dirty restrooms, and litter are among the top instrumental attributes listed. The responses are still a minority of 25 to 30 of the tourists, but they cannot be ignored.

In reviewing the expectations of visiting tourists, parking at the picnic area and visitor center are listed as first and second in their list of expectations. This may explain to some extent why parking appeared as a top-rated attribute despite its instrumental function. The remaining expectations are oriented toward expecting historical and specific event information leading up to the battle, as well as expecting displayed artifacts that also serve to inform. Yet, places to sit and rest also appear in the list of top-10 expectations. As with Castillo de San Marcos, it is clearly important that visiting tourists have sufficient seating for resting and just absorbing their surroundings. This appears to be an important design feature that can be easily overlooked when the focus of engineers and planners is geared toward the museum displays and exhibits. For the most part, the expressive and instrumental ratings continue a similar pattern as in the above park surveys. Data comprising this survey are found in the study by Floyd (1993b).

Cape Lookout National Seashore

Geographically, the park is comprised of a long, thin chain of sandy islands on the North Carolina coast that range from Beaufort inlet in the southeast to Ocracoke in the northeast. The seashore is a mix of bare, sandy beaches and sparse, mixed vegetation and a dune system off the beach covered in sea oats and salt meadow grass. Behind that the interior backs up to a large system of salt marches on the bay side of the seashore. The ocean side is a sea turtle nursery including the endangered loggerhead.

The seashore provides recreational activities from shelling, sunbathing, backpacking, and primitive camping. In the coastal waters, boating, fishing, and sea kayaking are available. In the fall, sport fishing is popular. Cabins and campsites are also available for extended stays. The island chain is connected by several ferry companies. Several historic sites such as a lighthouse and keeper's quarters and Portsmouth village are part of the seashore.

The ratings of attributes by tourists to Shackleford Banks find that of the 30 characteristics listed, the top attributes are expressive. They include the swimming area, friendliness of the staff, birdwatching, camping, fishing, shell collecting, cast netting, and overall appearance. The bottom-rated attributes tend to be instrumental dealing with the availability of waste containers, shade shelters, picnic tables, restrooms, and the availability of quality drinking water. The rating of the Core Banks, Portsmouth Village, the Historic Lighthouse, and Keepers Quarters follows a similar pattern, with the expressive receiving the highest ratings and the instrumental faring the most poorly.

The perceptions of problems by the tourists are minimal with the vast majority of surveyed attributes listed as "not a concern." As Floyd (1993a, p. 23) notes in the report: "respondents did not encounter many of the problems listed in the questionnaire." Not enough waste containers, litter, insects, and cleanliness are the attributes listed with the highest concern. Again, as in the above studies, these attributes tend to be instrumental in function.

In reviewing the responses to the 36 attributes listed as expectations of tourists visiting the seashore, the top expected attributes tend to be instrumental. Floyd (1993a, pp. 17-23) indicates that six park attributes are "definitely not expected. They include more beach rentals, people acting out how life was at the lighthouse, a place staging local events, lifeguards and protected beaches, and a museum with light and visual displays." Other attributes not generally expected include food and drink services.

In extrapolating those attributes that are definitely expected or very definitely expected by the visiting tourists, at least 30% include seeing displays of old costumes, adequate parking, information about life on the Outer Banks, museum-display items from the past, showcases of historic and natural artifacts, more information on the area, fewer vehicles, more restrooms, places with scenic vistas, and general park information. To a lesser degree, places to sit and rest, picnic areas, more trash containers, and walking-climbing areas are expected.

Floyd (1993a, p. 23) reports that "expectations are in line with the kinds of services and facilities available at the park." In reviewing the data, perceived problems and expectations concerning litter and not enough trash containers stand out as major issues of the visiting public. Increased attention to this matter by the park staff through their interpretative and information programs can help correct this situation, which again is an instrumental function. Data for this review are found in a report of a site survey by Floyd (1993a).

Gulf Islands National Seashore

Located on the Mississippi gulf coast, the park is composed of barrier islands, sandy beaches, coastal marshes, and bayou. This study focuses on tourists to Fort Massachusetts on Ship Island. The site offers the best opportunities for primitive camping, fishing, boating, swimming, picnicking, hiking, and visiting an historic fort and ruins. Fort Massachusetts is mainly reached by private individual and excursion boat tours from Gulfport and Biloxi. The fort and Ship Island provide attributes that offer a full range of tourist qualities to test a model.

In evaluating the ratings of the visitors to the island and fort, the average overall rating of satisfaction indicates that 89.4% of respondents rated the site good to excellent (Jurowski, Cumbow, Uysal, and Noe, 1995-6, p. 59). The attributes that are the most outstanding again follow the expressive-instrumental pattern. The excursion boat rides presenting an interpretative program about the Mississippi Sound and sea life, the tour of the fort, walking the island, the clean beaches and pier area, the swimming areas, and quality of water for swimming received high expressive ratings. The lower ratings tend to be instrumental attributes such as the picnic tables, sales items, drinking water, shade and shelter areas, and restrooms. At the fort area, the outdoor and guard room exhibits, although expressive attributes, also receive low ratings. Although these ratings still represent a small portion of the touring public, they cannot be discounted, only improved upon.

In reviewing the responses to problems as perceived by the touring public, the two top-rated problems deal with nature—too many insects and jellyfish. However, not enough shade areas at the beach, expensive food and souvenirs, not enough waste containers, restroom cleanliness, and insufficient visitor information can be corrected. In general, most of the perceptions of problems comprise a small minority of touring respondents except for the jellyfish problem, against which swimmers can be forewarned and proper topical astringent made available.

The expectations of the public are, for the most part, met by the facilities, services, and programs provided by the park staff. A few exceptions occur on a seasonal basis (Burchell, Hubble, and Ellard, 1991). For the winter and spring seasons, the tourists expected more food service, information, and exhibits. For the summer, the tourist respondents expected more information and exhibits; more conveniences such as drinking fountains, showers, and toilets; more shade; food service; and trash containers. During the fall, expectations are generally met except for tourists expecting more exhibits, information, and directional signs. The problem of information and exhibits seems to cross all seasons of the year and can be easily improved upon to meet tourist expectations. During the summer, seasonal increases in service areas are necessary. The Gulf Islands study also includes a test of how past experience with the site could alter subsequent expectations. The model suggests that the only significant impact is on expressive expectations from past experience. The moderate negative (Beta = –0.166) suggests that more frequent visits result in lower expressive expectations.

Overall satisfaction can be compromised by instrumental facilitators.

In analyzing the effects of the instrumental and expressive attributes on satisfaction, a LISREL path model was applied to analyze the variables so as to best select "the richest and most parsimonious model to explain the satisfaction process" (Jurowski, Cumbow, Uysal, and Noe, 1995-6, pp. 56, 65). In testing the efficacy of the various models, the final model resulting from this research implies that instrumental and expressive satisfiers work together to produce overall satisfaction. Marketing strategists must recognize that expressive expectations play an important role in the assessment of satisfaction while instrumental expectations alone are not nearly as important. However, overall satisfaction depends upon the acceptability of instrumental facilitators. Likewise, park managers concerned with the allocation of resources must be careful not to focus on either instrumental or expressive factors exclusively, in light of the interplay of these variables in influencing how park users evaluate their site experiences. Data resulting in this review and the article cited above by Jurowski et al. (1995-6) are based upon a survey and report by Burchell et al. (1991).

CONCLUSION

The current, working model of satisfaction that has evolved includes instrumental and expressive evaluative preferences, perceived site problems, and expectations. But this is not the final version, and additions and modifications are being planned even as this is being written. Obviously, the SERVQUAL attributes will play a role in future research into tourist situations. We suspect that reliability in the RATER model will be more associated with expressive attributes while responsiveness, assurance, empathy, and tangibles will be more related to the instrumental attributes.

Moreover, the significance of how a tourist values the benefits of an attribute is yet another factor that will need to be further measured through site surveys. An attribute may be highly rated but possess little value for the visiting tourist. It is important to simultaneously measure the rating, value, and expectation associated with an attribute and whether the touring public perceives an attribute to be a problem in facilitating an experience. Understanding what affects satisfaction is an open-ended proposition. Buchanan (1983, p. 40) argues that "if satisfaction is to provide usable information for managers and planners, an accurate understanding of the satisfactions associated with recreation participation as well as the factors which induce variability in those satisfactions must be clearly understood." While much has been done to further our understanding of satisfaction, still more field research needs to be accomplished through reliable and valid survey analysis.

In reviewing the above findings, the results tend to show skewness in the findings toward the positive, satisfaction end of the scale in ratings. This seems to be a situation associated with direct measures of satisfaction. Skewness repeatedly happens in satisfaction studies for most attribute items irrespective of the situation, but attribute items will emerge that reveal a customer's relative dissatisfaction. In reviewing numerous studies analyzing measurements of satisfaction, Hanan and Karp (1989, pp. 114-115) report "a high level of satisfaction exists if the top categories add up to between 85 and 95 percent. Average satisfaction ranks between 70 to 80 percent while anything under 60 percent is low." Dissatisfaction ratings "generally average below 50%." Except for a few attributes in the park cases, most of the survey respondents are generally satisfied. There are, however, attributes that need attention because of the high dissatisfaction ratings that are reported to be between 30 and 50%. But these are the exceptions in most cases because managers of tourist sites are not in the business of promoting dissatisfaction. Most managers and park rangers strive tirelessly to fulfil or exceed a customer's expectations and evaluations.

A pattern of expressive attributes takes the lead in providing satisfaction ratings, while instrumental attributes seem to take the lead in providing corresponding dissatisfaction ratings. These attribute distinctions are not to be thought of as categorically distinct, but rather as working together to reflect an overall evaluation. Future research will better clarify this relationship and how other attributes relate to this pattern.

*The problem of specification in measurement is essential
to understanding an attitude of satisfaction.*

■ 5

Measurement of Tourism Satisfaction

WHY A PHILOSOPHY OF SATISFACTION MEASUREMENT?

Input on Satisfaction Evaluation

NO TOURIST provider possesses unlimited resources to long ignore the customer's perceptions of what is acceptable or unacceptable, important or unimportant, desirable or undesirable that result in a customer being satisfied or dissatisfied. A belief about the significance of understanding customers' judgments and how to measure or gauge those opinions is fundamental to marketing a service, staying competitive, and remaining profitable.

Effective measurement techniques and methods are extremely important tools for the tourist provider in acquiring valid, reliable, and useful data. This chapter will touch on some of the basic issues in acquiring useful customer information, but for the most part it will deal with the larger methodological issue of why measuring satisfaction is a top priority. If there is one message that the reader can take away from this review it is that "customer satisfaction is not a remedial strategy. . . . It should be installed as the very genesis of a business" (Hanan and Karp, 1989, p. 23). The social science literature is replete with books and monographs detailing surveying and interviewing techniques including Ryan's (1995) text on researching tourist satisfaction. More generic texts and methodological material specializing in quantitative and qualitative research techniques are also available in the literature (Chakrapani, 1998). Scientific articles are also a growing source of information (Maddox, 1985). While few in number in the tourist and hospitality field, there are baseline works that change the way many providers do business. In their study of a San Francisco hotel, Barsky and Huxley (1992, p. 24) provide data to support that conducting a reliable and valid guest survey is essential to facilitate management decision making. By acquiring a "quality sample" as opposed to responses gathered from a non-survey sample guest card whose results are "generally unreliable and inaccurate, managers will learn more about who their customers really are and will, therefore, be more capable of serving and satisfying guests." The substance of this conclusion relies on the variables associated with a gap model that includes measures of expectation, importance, perceptions, and evaluative measures of satisfaction.

The customer is not a passive recipient, and responses either to negative or positive service experiences are not always voluntary. In identifying gaps in service quality among hotel guests, Bojanic (1996, p. 11) suggests "the first step in a service-quality management program is to identify the primary determinants of quality. In its simplest form, this type of information can be obtained by recording customer complaints and compliments." But this is just a first step and should be treated as a source for more randomized follow-up assessment. Many customers believe it does not pay to complain because since they are a single voice among so many, nothing will change. Some customers fear reprisal and confrontational interaction. Almanza, Jaffe, and Lin (1994, p. 66) find that in food service situations, "customers complain when the performance standard of an attribute is not met, but they do not provide compliments when that standard is exceeded." The key is to concentrate therefore on those attributes "that matter most to customers," irrespective of the source of the response. Praise or complaints are cues to what means most to a customer. Encouraging such interaction from the customer is a first step into the subjective realm that forms customer opinion. Attitudes and opinions are early warning signs that are often used to change negative services before they become debilitating to a tourist provider. "Attitudes become negative before sales actually decline, so attitudes can serve an important early warning function. Attitude analysis also helps identify key growth factions in a market that can act as the foundation for new sales" (Hanan and Karp, 1989, p. 107). Measuring attitudes and expectations is a crucial tool for understanding your comparative strengths and weaknesses measured against your competitors (Chon, 1989). Attitude measurement information can be the basis for enlarging and not just defending your market share when associated with concrete service attributes.

In measuring how attitudes are formed for tourist marketing strategies, first identify the attributes considered as being important; second, measure the importance of each attribute; and third, measure how much of that attribute is contained in the product or service. Applying empirical strategies that trace the salience of an attribute is considered to be an essential step in the process of understanding how an attitude toward a destination is formed. Mannell and Iso-Ahola (1987, p. 328) conclude that a measurement approach to the study of satisfaction is guided by the same fundamental approach in leisure and tourism studies. "Leisure and tourist researchers followed the same route. In the factor analytic studies, subjects have been presented with a large number of reasons and then asked to rate the importance of each reason for their leisure or touristic participation." In a survey of middle-aged, educated, upper-middle class international travelers living in New York, Goodrich (1977, 1978) applies an attitudinal model which assumes that a tourist's attitude to act is based on the perception of valued attributes and how important those attributes are held. The top five attributes perceived most important are (1) scenic beauty and sightseeing, (2) pleasant attitudes of the people, (3) availability of suitable accommodations, (4) opportunity for rest and relaxation, and (5) historic and cultural sites of interest. The results of the study show that preferences for tourist destinations are enhanced by favorable impressions and the attribute rank- ing of importance associated with a destination. Favorable attitudes of the tourist are essential in deciding on a travel destination. Once the major factors are deter- mined that lead to satisfaction in a tourist destination, then the next step is more microcosmic to define. The particulars of a service, facility, personnel, or program become the next target of inquiry. An assumption that most satisfaction approaches make is simply that "customer satisfaction is based on improvement. You must measure three things: (1) what you improve, (2) how much you improve it, and (3) how much better you improve it than your competitors" (Hanan and Karp, 1989, p. 99). In tourism research, the question of satisfaction begins by soliciting and analyzing responses from the public. Encouraging voluntary, substantive input pro- vides the basis for more systematic investigations. But a basic philosophy of acquir- ing data on a routine basis is fundamental to ensuring customer input. Satisfaction studies investigating how attitudes in relationship to service and situational cus- tomer responses led to the formation of favorable or unfavorable attitudes sets the stage for making improvements and adjusting service.

Special Facilitators of Satisfaction

When you hear them say that a ser- vice is exceptional and goes beyond their wildest expectations, you stop and take notice. However, the reality is simply that most of our experiences and expectations are not geared to that level of anticipa- tion. A poster hangs on the wall of a din- ing establishment for tourists and locals in a large, family-oriented restaurant near Williamsburg, Virginia. It is a picture of a work mule, and the caption reads: "I

> *The customer is not a passive recipient, and responses are not always voluntary either to negative or positive service experiences.*

ain't doin' quite as well as I expected, but then I never really expected I would." Most of us learn early in life that inflated expectations quickly usher in disappoint- ment, and our expectations are accordingly adjusted to more reasonable or moder- ate levels. The tourist provider needs to take advantage of ways to facilitate satisfac- tion by providing the traveler with a memorable experience that simply exceeds this threshold. To illustrate, Volk (1997, p. 12) recalls a particularly "sad" stay at a hotel in Boston's Copley Plaza, in a nonsmoking room with cigarette burns on the carpet, peeling paint, and a view of a ventilation duct. What she says exemplifies a finely honed set of expectations that set a personal standard: "I like to unwrap a pleated white paper from a French milled soap and take a tub with aromatic bath salts. I like sun streaming in through the windows, extra blankets in the closet, and not the pilly acrylic kind either. I like not having to say 'excuse me' to get past Andy [husband] and a place to put the luggage so you don't see it and can pretend you're living there. I like a magnifying mirror in the bathroom and the fuzzy feeling of being spoiled by a hotel. Isn't that the idea? Why leave home if you're leaving it for someplace worse?" That is precisely the idea, to be a little or a lot spoiled by the hospitality of the hotel, otherwise the comforts of home will do. The tourist provider is not helpless in responding to such expectations by recognizing that there are special facilitators to satisfaction that seem to work well in many diverse situations.

These facilitators of satisfaction are described in more detail elsewhere in this text, but they are worthy of being highlighted once more because they represent special avenues of behavior that can be used to make the customer king or queen for a stay. A tourist business that proudly but discreetly displays its philosophy of satisfaction will exhibit certain admirable traits.

First, the customer is top priority.

Saying this is redundant, but it needs to be said again for all in the hotel, hospitality, and tourism field. Do not underestimate the customer. "Satisfied customers are the essence of any successful ongoing enterprise. Trust, mutual respect, and a basic sense of integrity running through a company will find manifestation in the customer's awareness of the commitment the company has made to providing service on a grand scale" (Mahfood, 1993, p. 12). Always deliver the service that you promised. The appearance of the facilities and the employees should also be a demonstrable sign of commitment to that service. The customer needs to know that he is dealing with capable people who are responsive and empathic to his every need and concern. Facilities, services, programs, and personnel provide unique points of interaction for satisfying the customer. Above all else, learn what the customer expects from them, not only today, but continually monitor into the future. Find out and discover what the customer values, what he ranks as important in his experience. Assess what the customer selectively perceives, remembers, and recalls of the service offered. In essence, get to know your customer. When put into practice, such a business philosophy truly promotes satisfaction.

Second, listen to the customer.

Genuinely listen to what your customers are telling you. Encourage them to share their ideas on how facilities, services, and programs may be improved. This means evaluating both the instrumental and expressive attributes that make up a total service product. The principles of measurement should include letting your customers say what counts from their perception. "The first phase of a customer satisfaction research process should be to conduct personal interviews" (Hinton and Schaeffer, 1994, p. 43). Procedures should exist for tracking verbal communication of the customers when they render evaluative judgments about a service or lack thereof. Arranging through exit inquiries whether customers would be willing to be interviewed by telephone or by mail questionnaire about their stay is another way of identifying key attributes needing inquiry. After conducting initial, open-ended, follow-up interviews, then it is time to take the next step by constructing multiple complementary scales and measures to evaluate those perspectives and link actual survey results to changes (Davidow and Uttal, 1989, see Chapter 8). As a result, "effective listening enhances the probability of success" at this stage in an investigation (Berry et al., 1993, p. 3).

Third, surprise the customer.

Create an atmosphere of wonder, taking the lead from the Disney Corporation that has turned this idea into theme parks. It is all a matter of scale or degree on how far this idea is taken. Labone (1996) argues that wonder is a part of leisure that is constructed though social interaction and individual experiences that are defined by perceived freedom, intrinsic satisfaction, and positive reinforcement. What is intrinsically satisfying in free-time leisure is the experience of wonder created through a surprise. In Smith's (1994, p. 590) tourism-product model, the freedom of choice element implies not just choice, but also the potential for happy surprises and spontaneity. Attractions recognize the value of pleasant surprises. Epcot schedules unannounced performances including parades and appearances by Disney characters throughout the theme park. "These unanticipated [by the visitor] events give the visitor the feeling that he or she is very fortunate to be in the right place at the right time, and thus is gaining extra value from the visit." Such controlled surprises are necessary for achieving a reputation for superior service. "To reach these heights, companies must capitalize on opportunities to surprise their customers" (Berry et al., 1993, p. 14).

Fourth, tailor the service to the customer.

Personalize the experience where possible because this also heightens satisfaction. In this often shrinking, impersonal world, where taking a number and waiting for service is a mark of endurance, the customer is delighted when someone in the service sector takes an interest in his expectations. A Delta airline stewardess set the standard by saying that the passenger should be "treated like a guest in my own home." It is the little things that sometimes mean a lot when a person is away from home. Courteous staff who remember your name and where you reside and offer you a newspaper, complimentary fruit, coffee, refreshment, or candy instill a feeling of welcome as if "that customer" were expected. Yet, this is still a commercial business, so care should be given to keep responses in perspective. For example, Levenstein (1996, p. 12) reports on the overwhelming response he received from a Houston hotel, renowned for its accommodations, to something that he considered neither noncritical nor a serious flaw in the service. "The current fashion is to delight customers with service and responsiveness beyond expectations, and in this case beyond reason." The good intentions of the company are compromised to the point that he notes "their word processors work well enough to create the image of a personalized note." Rather than adding an element of sincerity, the multiple responses and trinkets appear "overeager to the point of hypocrisy." So care should be taken to equitably respond when personalizing a service or correcting a failure.

Fifth, reward the customer.

A little luxury goes a long way. "Luxuries add up. Enough of them, and you've got something substantial" (Volk, 1997, p. 14). The author is not *de facto* referring to extravagant or expensive displays or gifts, but extraordinary thoughts of kindness displayed through a service. The Osterrecihischer Hof in Salzburg provides little amenities that add up to luxurious rewards. Such amenities include a miniature Sachertorte with a ribbon representing the colors of the Austrian flag or a white linen mat at the side of the bed so your feet touch it first before "toeing into your slippers." Little things like a welcome note from the proprietor—not some faceless corporation, but a real person—help establish a bond with the customer. Such symbols that are not a commonplace occurrence for most of us communicate how genuinely the customer's patronage is appreciated. Such acts of thoughtful kindness are also good for the ego. Care should be used in allocating coupons and price promotions as rewards, for they do not attract the loyal customer. Instead, use your established customer base to reward and expand their purchase of your services or to introduce a new service by offering them the premium. In general, the above five facilitators of satisfaction stand out as very key points to measure relative to a tourist situation that centers on the customer as a person. Moreover, satisfaction cannot be measured without more long-term considerations of customer loyalty.

SATISFACTION WITHOUT LOYALTY LACKS POWER

Loyal customers are the profit engine of a company, and through repeat business often account for 80% of total sales volume and profit. On a five-point Likert scale, they are the high fives of satisfaction. The loyalist group constitutes a company's core of clients whose expectations are so exceeded that they become "missionaries or apostles for the company" (Bhote, 1996, p. 28). What gives credibility to the loyalty model, however, is not profit but the creation of value for the customer. "Loyalty is inextricably linked to the creation of value as both a cause and an effect" (Reichheld, 1996, pp. 20-21). As an effect, loyalty measures whether a company has delivered superior value through repeat use of a company's tourist services. As a cause, revenues and market share grow, while sustainable growth attracts more highly productive employees. Loyalty also produces customer-retention savings, and shareholders act more like partners to stabilize the company.

Companies that exhibit a willingness to promote customer loyalty and complete satisfaction adhere to the Golden Rule of doing unto others as you do unto yourself. Loyalty is about "humanistic values and principles of the kind people devote their lives to, outside work and sometimes on the job as well. People have always been far more motivated to devote energy to organizations with a service goal than to organizations that exist exclusively to make a buck" (Reichheld, 1996,

p. 28). This brings us back to a central premise in Chapter 3 that views tourism as a complex organization of assets. It means that the traveler is also an asset if loyalty and complete satisfaction are a goal. "To manage customers as assets, you must be able to value them as service assets. This means you must be able to quantify and predict customer duration and lifecycle cash flow" (Reichheld, 1996, p. 34). Lifecycle benefits generated from repeated purchases of a service over a number of years may provide sustained profit for a company if the company continually improves and adds value for the customer. Loyalty also creates value for a company if it properly targets the right kind of customer. Knowing what market niche best maximizes value for a company within the hotel hospitality and travel business means finding, nurturing, and catering to that customer. It is not just the satisfied customer who always counts. It is learning from the defectors who are dissatisfied or, worse, from satisfied customers who still leave. The value of a loyal customer translates onto an account ledger as a realization of a base profit, not only from repeat use, but also from referrals as loyal customers turn into advocates. Revenue growth is further realized by retaining customers and gaining new market share as others experience a superior level of service. And finally, revenues increase through cost savings because your customers become more efficient in dealing in a long-term relationship. They are also more willing to pay the higher price premiums that often result because your customer wants to insure a continued quality of service.

Customer loyalty implies retention of the right kind of customer. The goal is to make the tourist loyal because it is cheaper to serve an old friend of the family than to try to make a new one. To be an old friend of a corporate family, the customers must have an emotional stake in the business who repeatedly purchase a company's services. Perhaps in time, they will turn into advocates who recommend others to use the services. Targeting the correct customer for a tourist business requires understanding what market segments, demographics, and affinity groups will be most loyal to the service being offered. Reichheld (1996, pp. 63-116) points out that businesses which seriously attempt to know and understand their customer's group affiliations and social ties consistently exceed their customer's expectation. For example, a major credit card company found that professionals such as accountants, nurses, engineers, and other such white-collar workers possess a higher loyalty disposition. From this information, they also target professional and educational groups as additional sources of loyal customers.

Another way of targeting the right kind of consumer group is zeroing in on specific recreational activities that are part of a tourist complex. Resorts and hotels that are associated with offering specific customer-tourist activities such as gambling, sporting activities, theme parks, or spas are most likely to be affected by repeat business and customer loyalty retention. General sightseeing may be a one-time event in the travel plans of a tourist and is less sensitive to repeat business and customer loyalty, save for the hospitality options that may be located within a certain geographic region. Griffin (1995, pp. 9-10) presents an example of a New England ski resort that was spending all its time on tracking and dealing with new customers, and "was taking the satisfied customer for granted." To counter flat growth, management switched to a system of incentives that locked skiers into repeated visits during the ski season. Equipment is sold at cost, there are coupons and freebies, and if they participate in the instructional program, by the fourth lesson first-time skiers are more likely to become loyal customers. Even marginal tourist companies can profit by focusing on delivering a consistent quality product. Through consistency in marketing an image and making good on that promise, the Carnival Cruise line has "doubled repeat business" even though the majority of customers are still new to cruising. The "fun image" of the line is backed up by service that delivers on that promise through organized activities and services that provide amusement (Griffin, 1995, p. 65). But the main benefactors of loyalty are in the hospitality area. The Marriott recognized that many of its guests are repeat users, so it started an employee empowerment program in 1988 to ensure immediate customer satisfaction. The Marriott knows that if just eight guests out of the thousands who spend more than five to seven nights per year with them leave and do not return that is one million dollars in lost sales.

Having identified the right kind of customers, the next step is retaining their patronage. In minimizing customer-tourist defection, companies should start with defection prevention. They should assign their top marketing personnel and problem solvers, overseen by a chief customer officer, to do the following: (1) Direct employees to intervene on behalf of the customer. (2) Monitor changes in drops in sales to determine the reasons for such shortfalls. (3) Establish a data-gathering network to obtain customer input, especially from those employees who come in contact with the customer, and act on their observations. (4) Establish quality standards that meet what it takes to achieve complete customer satisfaction so that retention rates remain stable and grow with the customer base. And (5) see to it that all employees are empowered and know that the customer is the company's most important asset. Above all, remember that the "most important elements of customer enthusiasm are those elements which the customer stresses as important" (Bhote, 1996, p. 47).

Despite the known consequences of losing customers, attrition is rampant throughout the industry. Reichheld (1996, p. 1) observes that "on average, U.S. corporations now lose half their customers in five years, half their employees in four, and half their investors in less than one." The consequences of this disloyalty result in stunted growth. Corporate performance is stunted by 25 to 50%, sometimes more. By contrast, businesses that concentrate on finding and keeping good customers, productive employees, and supportive investors continue to generate superior results. Dissatisfied customers are just as important as those who are completely satisfied because they defect to competition. "Letting such customers defect is perhaps one of the worst mistakes managers can make. Showering attention on them when problems strike can convert at least 50% of them to loyalists" (Bhote, 1996, p. 29). But management must be aggressive in facing up to problems. For example, AmeriSuites Hotel in Irving, Texas, is strategically located to serve a business located in the same neighborhood but lost the account. In contacting that company about why they left, AmeriSuites management determined specifically the kinds of problems that existed with the kind of service they offered. When the problems were corrected, they arranged a meeting and a demonstration to show how these issues were resolved. As a result, they won back the account. Griffin (1995, p. 201) enumerates seven points for winning back the customer. First, ask the question of how you can win back a client's business and trust. Second, listen closely to what they tell you. Third, meet the customer's requirements, and communicate that those changes were made. Fourth, be patient and open with the customer since it takes time to heal an injury. Fifth, stay in touch with the lost customer. Sixth, make it easy for the customer to return—peace offerings help. Seventh, when the customer returns, continue to earn his business every day. Part of earning that business is putting satisfaction scores and data in a proper context so that they truly address the specific instrumental and expressive needs of the customers and their expectations. Relying on satisfaction scores in a vacuum is not the answer. There is a proper role for satisfaction scores, and a common mistake to be avoided is in their application.

> **Companies that exhibit a willingness to promote customer loyalty and complete satisfaction adhere to the Golden Rule of doing unto others as you do unto yourself.**

Tourist companies need to be aware of the satisfaction trap, as Reichheld (1996, pp. 234-239) sees it, in which a company makes the customer-satisfaction ratings an end goal. "It's not that satisfaction doesn't matter; it matters a great deal. It's the manner, context, and priority of satisfaction measurement that has become a problem. And the problem is that if we fail to link satisfaction scores to customer loyalty and profits, they can all too easily become an end in themselves. In some organizations, they are considered a higher goal than profit."

This text does not advocate such a mindless exercise nor narrow confine for satisfaction scores. It is not enough to brag about one's high J.D. Power Satisfaction score in and of itself. "Companies can avoid the satisfaction trap if they remember that what matters is not how satisfied they keep their customers, but how many satisfied and profitable customers they keep" (Reichheld, 1996, p. 239). The management of a tourist company cannot afford to be complacent by just relying upon satisfaction scores. Griffin (1995, pp. 2-3) also reports that "satisfaction levels do not necessarily translate into higher sales and profits." The disparity is partially due to the way in which satisfaction is measured. Often, there is no linking of evaluations to price, changing value, or future anticipated behavior of the customer. For example, "customers who respond to price cutting may churn orders, but they seldom become loyal customers. They buy from whatever vendor offers the lowest price" (Griffin, 1995, p. 7). Price is a factor generally found to be least satisfying among customers. The quality and price of a service are important factors for producing tourist value, but they are not adequate to differentiate a company's services from that of their competition. The quality of a service must be translated into complete customer satisfaction. "Even in the 1990s, however, fewer than one-third of all companies have a comprehensive customer satisfaction focus" (Bhote, 1996, p. 6). Yet, companies must go beyond just satisfying the customer: they must "delight customers and earn their loyalty—often for life." This means that a tourist company must create "excitement" and "wow." In more specific terminology: "it reaches for features and services (attributes both expressive and instrumental) that customers have not expected or anticipated but which thrill them and raise their loyalty quotient" (Bhote, 1996. p. 9). To illustrate, "the Sheraton Towers Hotel in Singapore is an excellent example of how offering the unexpected generates customer delight and subsequent loyalty. When you enter the lobby, the bellhop does not take you to the registration desk but directly to an assistant manager who, surprisingly, already knows your name. With no waiting in line, you are ushered into your room. Moments later, a butler comes in to check if everything is to your satisfaction, and offers to press your clothes and shine your shoes free of charge. Someone else brings in a whole complimentary case of toiletries. In the afternoon, a snack is served with your tea. You are invited to join the general manager in the evening for free cocktails and hors d'oeuvres. The night ends with a rich dessert served in your room before bedtime. Wake-up calls come with free tea or coffee and morning newspaper of your choice. The staff on your floor greet you by name. That is the difference between customer satisfaction and customer delight" (Bhote, 1996, p. 50).

Just operating at an intermediate level of customer satisfaction will not be sufficient to guarantee loyalty. Bhote (1996, p. 31) argues that because customer loyalty and satisfaction are weakly correlated, it is no longer customer satisfaction but customer loyalty that is the dominant key to business success. By that he means "customers are so delighted with a company's product or service that they become enthusiastic word-of-mouth advertisers." However, at the highest level of customer satisfaction, strong attitudinal support is found to reinforce repeat business. It appears not to be just a matter of either satisfaction or loyalty, but rather a matter of sufficiently boosting and increasing satisfaction levels to their maximum potential to insure loyalty. Bhote (1996, p. 39) reports a "strong link between customer retention and customer profit and between complete customer satisfaction and customer loyalty." He quotes Horst Schulze, president and CCO (Chief Customer Officer) of the Ritz-Carlton Hotel, to reinforce that premise. "Unless you have 100% customer satisfaction—and I don't mean that they are just satisfied but are excited about what you are doing—you have to improve. And even if you reach 100% customer satisfaction, you have to make sure that you listen just in case they change—so that you can change with them." Travel and tourist companies must be sensitive to what a customer is telling them and strive to achieve outstanding customer ratings to guarantee repeat business or avoid destructive public opinion. It absolutely requires pushing satisfaction ratings to their highest level. The conclusions are real: "Loyal customers provide higher profits, more repeat business, higher market share, and more referrals," and "totally satisfied customers are six times more likely to repurchase a company's products over a span of one to two years than merely satisfied customers." Finally, those 2% of the companies that believe in maximizing customer satisfaction are able to document "those bottom-line improvements" (Bhote, 1996, p. 145). This is the challenge for a tourist-related company, but there are extraneous social forces that intervene to disconnect a customer from a tourist provider no matter how good a service.

Circumstances beyond the control of a company are always poised to derail the tourist-customer, and those who disconnect may even include customers who are completely satisfied or delighted. The fact is, the world changes and so do the customers living in it. The most loyal patrons will defect if the tourist provider does not fulfil their emerging new needs, if new markets develop that provide more innovative values, and finally, if there are negative changes in the political or economic environment as perceived by the customer and tourist community. Baloglu and Erickson (1998) also investigated the process of normal switching behavior among mostly competing multiple destinations. Their findings show that most of the international visitors of one destination are more likely to switch to another destination for their next trip. The size of the actual loyal group of tourists was small compared to those who preferred to switch. In the countries compared, once travelers visited Italy, Turkey, and Greece, they visited Egypt. This suggests that travelers visit destinations in an orderly sequence within a contiguous frame of reference. For the most part, loyalty issues in tourism research have focused on those factors which determine loyalty (Backman and Crompton, 1991a, 1991b), and how loyalty manifests itself among travelers (Pritchard and Howard, 1997).

The decision of tourists in choosing recreational travel is not a zero-sum decision, whether they either fly a particular airline, stay in a particular hotel or a particular resort, or do not act. During a lifetime, tourists will make many decisions about recreational travel but they may not always use a particular set of assets. Loyalty tied to a profit model of repeat visits, year in and year out, is a goal, not an absolute given cast in stone. In attempting to achieve high levels of customer satisfaction and loyalty, a solid program should always be built on and guided by a strong consumer-information base that monitors and anticipates change. The next section takes up some of the issues associated with designing and constructing a formal database to monitor satisfaction and retention of tourist customers.

APPROACHES TO TOURIST MEASUREMENT

Measurement Strategies

As part of a measurement philosophy, a general orientation or goal toward directing an applied research effort needs to be clearly stated, not in methodological terms, but in management terms. Applied customer research is not an afterthought, but should be part of the ongoing decision-making process that directs how management resources are to be spent on providing a satisfactory service. Satisfaction data on the customer should and must be useful in three ways (Hinton and Schaeffer, 1994, p. 58). The data should be the ongoing "base for a trend analysis," a "basis for prioritizing actions for improvement," and "keys to setting goals." Expectations change in a dynamic market. As services improve, expectations tend to migrate upward, and then the provider must anticipate or lose market. Since attitudes change before customers walk, customer data are a sure way a tourist provider has of realistically anticipating such shifts in preference. "The purpose of measuring client satisfaction is to get the client's mental report card in writing" (Cottle, 1990, p. 97). It is an attempt to quantify subjective responses to a limited set of service parameters that the tourist provider has some control over such as services, facilities, programs, and personnel.

A valid and reliable measurement program that yields explanations and understanding should include certain steps that are vigorously followed. First, "conducting a service quality study is analogous to taking a snapshot. Deeper insight and an understanding of the pattern of change comes from taking many snapshots from multiple angles" (Berry et al., 1993, p. 2). Conducting satisfaction studies about service attributes is not a one-time event. It is a commitment to a continual process of assessment, evaluation, and review to be successful. Second, in setting up your measurement scales, you need to ask, "what are the values our people must deliver?" The customers' "must list" will give you the answer (Hanan and Karp, 1989, p. 123). What the customers value most about a service is the basis for building and directing a service. The customer is always right in deciding what satisfies him. Third, "market segmentation is important to the success of your survey." Two typical segmentation methods are grouping customers by demographics and social group characteristics or by function and experience (Hinton and Schaeffer, 1994, p. 47; Jurowski, Uysal, and Noe, 1993). Segmentation data provide information for promotional efforts, are estimating the size and impact of a market, and stimulate service developments that appeal to a particular market niche. Fourth, relying on any single approach to data gathering often leads to premature closure and lost input. Lytle (1993, pp. 52-64) finds common measurement mistakes among companies trying to assess their customers' needs, perceptions, and expectations. They tend to unduly rely on closed-ended research, do their own in-house assessments, or listen solely to the results of focus groups or personal interviews. Unfortunately, Lytle endorses telephone interviews that have their own set of shortcomings. If anything, no one technique is more appropriate than another to get the job done. It takes a battery of various scales and techniques to assure quality customer satisfaction data. Locking a measurement program into a single or very limited set of measurement options is a poor philosophy, since it overlooks the particular nuances of a situation. As a young researcher in the early '70s, I will never forget the judgment of a manager in the Great Smoky Mountains National Park who pointedly told me that "their visitors" are different than other national park visitors. What he was reacting against was the cookie-cutter belief among some researchers then, and still today, that one instrument, one approach, one set of attributes, one set of SES (socioeconomic items), and one set of attitude questions are all anyone needs to deal with the customer. This belief was wrong then and still is today. It was an invaluable lesson to learn.

Whatever research measurements are finally adopted in dealing with customer satisfaction, it begins and ends with the customer. The principles of measurement should include letting your customers say what matters from their perceptions. But "masters of customer service know that research begins with open-ended questions" (Davidow and Uttal, 1989, p. 76). With that approach, British Airways not only discovered that their passengers sought to be treated with care and concern, but also learned how their personnel were resolving passenger problems. Especially, how flexible they were in applying company policy and their ability to recover from mistakes were two areas that customers volunteered substantive information, which was an unexpected bonus. In the initial stages of any research, inquiry should include as wide as possible a range of input from the customer and manager. Contacting customers is always a measurement issue. Naumann (1995, p. 168) suggests some interesting ways of gathering data by:

(1) Involving top management interaction with customers to informally sample views over time.
(2) Involving customers in open house meetings with staff and management.
(3) Involving the customer at the idea stage in new and proposed service development.
(4) Involving customers in experimental prototype services in test sites.
(5) Involving customer panels on changing needs.
(6) Involving customers with a company's internal quality teams to discuss pertinent problems and issues. A systematic gathering of this kind of input establishes a foundation upon which to construct more closed-ended items that can be used with a larger sample population of customers.

In closing, one of the biggest mistakes companies make is not looking at their competition. It is sad to say, but true, that "understanding customers' views of your competitors is there for the asking, but few ask" (Hinton and Schaeffer, 1994, p. 51). Valuable insight is gained by comparing, from the perspective of your customer, how another company services the same or a similar market. The goal is simply to obtain insight into what the customers value most and what satisfies them the most in considering a tourist service. A philosophy of instituting a customer research approach starts with a process of deciding how to systematically gather valid, reliable, and useful information intended to change, modify, and even revolutionize a service delivery system in tourism. Having made that decision, the next step is choosing certain types of scales and techniques to represent that information in such a way that those comparisons can be made between the satisfied and dissatisfied customer. There are options available to the researcher, and issues associated with certain choices that need to weighed.

Measurement Options

In selecting measures for determining customer satisfaction, Cannie and Caplin (1991, pp. 104-106) warn against relying on management intuition to ascertain customer needs. They suggest obtaining three kinds of objectively managed data that focus on opportunity, strategic, and evaluational information. Questionnaire or interview items need to be developed that look at unlocking new opportunities or emerging expectations. Travelers told Holiday Inn researchers that they would like to find a familiar service in an unfamiliar location, so Holiday Inn came up with a 1-800 phone service to meet that new expectation among their guests.

The second type of information items deals with strategic information that should tell management where they can better focus financial and human resources to serve the needs of all their clients, not just a select segment. National park tourists told researchers that litter is more tolerated in service locations such as restrooms or picnic areas than elsewhere in a park. As a result, management diverted rangers and field personnel to the trails and natural situations where there is little or no tolerance for litter.

And finally, evaluative-information items seek to measure customer perceptions of ongoing services dealing with the daily operations of an organization that is seen as being more or less satisfying or dissatisfying. For example, an airport information system, although effective and positively evaluated in large public areas, is not readily accessible in other remote passenger locations. These systems can be easily relocated to increase effectiveness. The National Park Service learned that gas station attendants along a parkway are alternate sources of park information for the public. All information does not flow from a visitor center. Sometimes the most seemingly mundane jobs take on the most significance. Walt Disney Production invests four full weekdays in training new ticket takers. They recognize that most probably the first Disney employee a customer interacts with is a ticket taker. The tourist will be asking questions on where to go, how to get there, and what to experience next. Moreover, they will expect a courteous, correct, and timely reply. These trainee ticket takers also learn about dealing with their "Guests" with a capital G. The Disney Corporation impresses upon their employees the significant status held by the visiting public.

Seeking information that searches out new opportunities, or information that redirects where resources are better used, is worthwhile when organized on a scientific basis. In essence, to ensure world-class, reliable, and valid information, it must be neutrally gathered and accurately measured. The customer's input is gathered through surveys, questionnaires, focus groups, and also less formal approaches that frequently tie in an award, gift, or premium as an incentive to participate. Customer-oriented items or questions should reflect a customer's perceptions and be organized in an instrument as closely as possible to the order of his experience as if each experience possessed an entrance and exit. Ask customers to rate current services and solicit options for improvement. Try to identify held expectations and current values associated with the service. Finally, find what may be missing and what it takes to exceed their expectations. For a very clear technical overview on details involving data-gathering and benchmarking approaches and practices see Barsky (1995). Management insight is never a substitute for scientifically organized customer interviews. Suggestion boxes, comment cards, or "how are we doing" approaches are mere afterthoughts to fill up the blank spaces on a receipt. There is no substitute for objective information.

No matter what type of objective research approaches are applied to data gathering, Hinton and Schaeffer (1994, pp. 52-56) warn against eight common measurement shortcomings that can seriously confound the integrity of the findings and limit measurement findings.

(1) "You can't make the data answer a question that you didn't ask." Such situations are common after the fact but of little help when you need to evaluate specific relationships.

(2) "Typically, valid conclusions cannot be drawn from data which are segmented differently from the original sample drawn." Know in advance what population, social psychological, regional, cultural, or personality variables that might explain a relationship should be part of the survey instrument.

> The purpose of measuring client satisfaction is to get the client's mental report card in writing.

(3) "Don't force fit data or stretch research results to prove a point." The national press calls this cooking the data, and it has cost individuals their careers and professional reputations. There is no forgiveness for such an error of judgment.

(4) "Don't assume an average score means that you are average." Look at the distributions, look at the numbers, and look at the way scales are summed because an average can hide extremes.

(5) "Be sure that the person who uses or attempts to use sophisticated analysis techniques understands the power and the limitations of those techniques." There are some very powerful parametric multivariate techniques that have some equally powerful assumptions that must be met before they can be legitimately applied to a data set. There are also nonparametric techniques that are often overlooked when they would do nicely for rank order or interval data. Statistics are tools, a means to an end, not the final word.

(6) "If you must use data from a survey which is not up to date, proceed with caution. Try to validate the survey's present relevance and accuracy." Historical data can baseline a trend but it is always wise to determine where on the curve that information lies.

(7) "Don't view the research on a stand-alone basis only. Blend it with other information." Remember, a study merely reduces the uncertainty. It proves nothing in and of itself. Multiple studies bring more confidence to the results because the uncertainty is further reduced.

(8) "Look at the data by customer or customers as well as the real frequency or need" for the service. Travelers may only require a service during a part of a

trip. Don't assume, because it is so infrequently used, it has no place. At some point laundry must be cleaned, and medical service may be required.

In deciding on what kind of scale or measurement option to use in obtaining customer responses, there are few rules in measuring customer satisfaction. Quantifiable data are needed at least at the interval level. Cottle (1990, pp. 99, 108-109) recommends a five- or seven-point unbalanced scale and strongly decries a nominal yes/no response format. A seven-point differential scale with bipolar ends of "greatly exceeds expectations vs. greatly falls short of expectations" is an easily handled quantitative format. Matched pairs of judgments based on the perception as well as expectation will also give a more complete picture (Parasuraman, Zeithaml, and Berry, 1984, 1994). Turning a dyad of a matched pair into a triad and adding the importance of an attribute more completely measures satisfaction or dissatisfaction. In the end, evaluating the effectiveness of customer satisfaction scales, Griffin and Hauser (1992, p. 36) find no "single best measure" on either a six-, nine-, 10-, or 100-point scale in testing products. Whether this holds for service categories remains an open question. Hanan and Karp (1989, pp. 114-115) analyze measurements of satisfaction on a Likert scale. They conclude that a high level of satisfaction exists if the top categories add up to between 85 and 95%. Average satisfaction ranks from 70 to 80% while anything under 60% is considered low. Resulting bottom scale negatives are formed by adding the two bottom categories that generally average well below 50%. Whatever scale size is used seems appropriate, if it is an unbalanced one with a neutral midpoint to differentiate between the choices. Whatever the choice, the consequences remain: "there is no guarantee of a satisfied customer's repeat visit, but it is nearly certain that a dissatisfied customer will not return" (Dube, Renaghan, and Miller, 1994, p. 39).

CONCLUSION

Customer data gathering is not a haphazard activity but rather a systematic process that requires organizational and management support. Financial funding is a prerequisite, but management's support does not stop with simply underwriting customer surveys. A basic and fundamental commitment to understanding how best to satisfy the customer is the cornerstone of any good management policy. Whatever data-gathering system is followed, as long as it is grounded solidly on valid and reliable survey procedures, people will have confidence in it. If the information provides insight into areas of customer concern where positive changes can be implemented, then its usefulness is assured; if such data are routinely consulted and put to the test by being applied in the daily operations of an organization, confidence will grow that change is truly driven by the perceptions, expectations, and valuations of the customer.

In the review of surveys in the previous chapter, it is evident that the initial model changed substantially with subsequent tests. As new ideas and different theories of satisfaction continue to be integrated into the most recent research, modification continues. Changes are part of the future as new ways of testing and analyzing data that hope to improve understanding and the ability to predict and explain are introduced. Changes are usually evaluated by experimenting with new techniques and evaluating their merit independently before any wholesale institutionalization of them occurs. Research to try different ideas within the applied nature of the work is an accepted practice to be encouraged and rewarded.

The best kind of customer research is also driven by experimentation that directly demonstrates the utility of such data-gathering efforts among customers and employees. A prototype for the organization is changed and compared against what is the daily norm. In one case study of a national park, it became very evident from the database that "sightseeing" consistently showed up as a major customer interest. In fact, some surveys at the national level further confirmed that sightseeing perhaps accounted for most of the park visitation. Since maintaining a park, its roads, and its natural resources is costly and labor intensive, one superintendent who managed a parkway decided to look at changing the grooming practices along that parkway. In a number of surveys, photo simulations, and video simulations, different points of comparison could be examined for the first time among parkway visitors. To measure those particular judgments about what the park visitor finds satisfying or dissatisfying, different visual situations are realistically manipulated, and then put to the test using conventional cross-sectional surveys. More recently, desktop computer visual simulations displaying realistic images are being used to test various maintenance and land-use practices. Instead of the employee with the gang mower, bush hog, or chainsaw ruling the day, the park visitor's input sets limits on practices (Noe and Hammitt, 1988). It is becoming more commonplace that hotels and resorts experiment with different room layouts and furnishing, just as the food services try new menus and decor. By taking the lead in trying different ideas, innovations can be modified or abandoned before the costs of introducing a new service are incorporated into the daily operations of a business.

A customer-satisfaction program embodies a discovery process that should never stop. The perceptions, expectations, and valuations of customers change as they grow and the world grows around them. What does not change is the central role of a customer. The customer is the most important person in a business. Finally, the customer brings to the tourist provider anticipation of a satisfactory experience waiting to be filled. Hopefully, a reliable and valid database is available to help anticipate and satisfy that request.

■ References

Allport., F.H. (1924). *Social psychology*. Boston: Houghton Mifflin.

Almanza, B.A., Jaffe, W., and Lin, L. (1994). Use of the service attribute matrix to measure consumer satisfaction. *Hospitality Research Journal, 17*(2):63-74.

Andrews, F.M., and Withey, S.B. (1976). *Social indicators of well being*. New York: Plenum Press.

Aveni, A. (1980). *Rambling raft race*. [Report]. Atlanta, GA: National Park Service, Southeast Regional Office.

Backman, S.J., and Crompton, J.L. (1991a). Differentiating between high, spurious, latent, and low loyalty participants in two leisure activities. *Journal of Park and Recreation Administration, 9*(2),1-17.

Backman, S.J., and Crompton, J.L. (1991b). The usefulness of selected variables for predicting activity loyalty. *Leisure Sciences, 13*, 205-220.

Baloglu, S., and Erickson, R.E. (in press). Destination loyalty and switching behavior of travelers: A Markov analysis. *Tourism Analysis*.

Barsky, J.D. (1992). Customer satisfaction in the hotel industry: Meaning and measurement. *Hospitality Research Journal, 16*(1), 51-73.

Barsky, J.D. (1995). *World-class customer satisfaction*. New York: Irwin.

Barsky, J.D., and Huxley, S.J. (1992, December:18-25). A customer-survey tool: Using the quality sample. *The Cornell H.R.A. Quarterly*.

Barsky, J.D., and Labagh, R. (1992, October: 32-40). A strategy for customer satisfaction. *The Cornell H.R.A. Quarterly*.

Bartlett, P., and Einert, A.E. (1992). Analysis of the design function of an adult softball complex in a new public recreation park. *Journal of Park and Recreation Administration, 10*(1), 71-81.

Beard, J., and Ragheb, M. (1979). *Measuring Leisure Satisfaction*. Paper presented at the SPRE Research Symposium, National Recreation and Park Association, New Orleans, LA.

Beard, J., and Ragheb, M. (1980). Measuring leisure satisfaction. *Journal of Leisure Research,12*(1), 20-33.

Bearden, W.O., and Teel, J.E. (1983). Selected determinants of consumer satisfaction and complaint reports. *Journal of Marketing Research, 20*, 21-28.

Berry, L.L., and Parasuraman, A. (1991). *Marketing services*. New York: Free Press.

Berry, L.L., Parasuraman, A., and Zeithaml, V.A.(1993). *Ten lessons for improving service quality*. (Report No. 93-104). Cambridge, MA: Marketing Science Institute.

Bhote, K.R. (1996). *Beyond customer satisfaction to customer loyalty*. New York: AMA Membership Publications Division

Bojanic, D.C. (1996). Consumer perceptions of price, value and satisfaction in the hotel industry: an exploratory study. *Journal of Hospitality & Leisure Marketing, 4*(1), 5-22.

Bojanic, D.C., and Rosen, L.D. (1994). Measuring service quality in restaurants: an application of the SERVQUAL instrument. *Hospitality Research Journal, 18*(1), 3-14.

Bornstein, G., Milliken, J.D., and Fitzgibbon, J. (1985). *Moore Park: A study in visual and recreational preferences* (Major paper). Ontario, Canada: University of Guelph, School of Landscape Architecture, The Library Business Office, McLaughlin Library.

Brown, B.A., and Frankel, G.B. (1993). Activity through the years: Leisure, leisure satisfaction, and life satisfaction. *Sociology of Sport Journal, 10*(1), 1-17.

Bryden, J., and Faber, M. (1971). Multiplying the tourist multiplier. Social and *Economic Studies, 20*(1), 61-82.

Buchanan, T. (1983). Toward an understanding of variability in satisfactions within activities. *Journal of Leisure Research, 15*(1), 39-51.

Burchell, C.L., Hubble, S.M., and Ellard, J.A. (1991). *Gulf Islands National Seashore* (Report). Atlanta, GA: National Park Service, Southeast Regional Office.

Burnaby, T.V., Swart, W.W., and Gearing, C.E. (1975). Management science and operations research in travel and tourism. *Review of Tourism, 30*(4),129-42.

Cannie, J.K. (1994). *Turning lost customers into gold*. New York: Amacom.

Cannie, J.K., and Caplin, D. (1991). *Keeping customers for life*. New York: Amacom.

Carr, J.A. (1990). Trends in tourism market research. *Trends, 27*(3), 10-13.

Center for Public and Urban Research, G.S.U. (1987). *Blue Ridge Parkway* (Report). Atlanta, GA: National Park Service, Southeast Regional Office.

Chadee, D.D., and Mattsson, J. (1996). An empirical assessment of customer satisfaction in tourism. *Service Industries Journal, 16*(3), 305-20.

Chakrapani, C. (1998). *How to measure service quality and customer satisfaction: The informal field guide for tools and techniques*. Chicago: American Marketing Institute.

Chon, K.S. (1989). Understanding recreational traveler's motivation, attitude, and satisfaction. *Tourist Review, 44*(1), 3-6.

Cohen, E. (1972). Toward a sociology of international tourism. *Social Research, 39*(1), 164-182.

Cohen, E. (1974). Who is a tourist: a conceptual clarification. *Sociological Review, 22*(4), 527-555.

Cohen, E. (1979). A phenomenology of tourist experiences. *Sociology, 13*, 179-201.

Connelly, N.A. (1987). Critical factors and their threshold for camper satisfaction at two campgrounds. *Journal of Leisure Research, 19*(3), 159-73.

Cooper, D. (1994). Portraits of paradise: themes and images of the tourist industry. *Southeast Asian Journal of Social Science, 22*(1), 144-60.

Cottle, D.W. (1990). *Client-centered service: How to keep them coming back for more.* New York: John Wiley & Sons.

Crompton, J.L., and Mackay, K.J. (1988). Users' perceptions of the relative importance of service quality dimensions in selected public recreation programs. *Leisure Sciences, 11,* 367-375.

Csikszentmchalyi, M. (1981). Leisure and socialization. *Social Forces, 60*(2), 135-138.

Czepiel, J.A., and Rosenberg, L.J. (1977). The study of consumer satisfaction: Assessing the "so what" question. In K.H. Hunt, *Conceptualizations and measurement of consumer satisfaction and dissatisfaction* (Report No. 77-103). Cambridge, Mass: Marketing Science Institute.

Davidow, W.H., and Uttal, B. (1989). *Total customer service.* New York: Harper & Row.

Day, G.S. (1993). *The capabilities of market-driven organizations.* (Report No. 93-123), Cambridge, MA: Marketing Science Institute.

De Rose, L.J. (1994). *The value network.* New York: Amacom.

Dillman, D. (1978). *Mail and telephone surveys: The total design method.* New York: Wiley.

Dimanche, F., Havitz, M.E., and Howard, D.R. (1991). Testing the involvement profile (IP) scale in the context of selected recreational and touristic activities. *Journal of Leisure Research, 23*(1), 51-66.

Ditton, R.B., Fedler, A.J.,and Graefe, A.R. (1981, October). *Motive importance commonalties as a basis for assessing recreational satisfaction.* Paper presented at the NRPA Annual Congress, Minneapolis, Minnesota.

Ditton, R.B.,Graefe A.R., and Fedler, A.J. (1979). *Recreational satisfaction at Buffalo National River: Some measurement concerns.* Paper presented at the Second Conference on Scientific Research in the National Parks, San Francisco, CA.

Dorfman, P.W. (1979). Measurement and meaning of recreation satisfaction. *Environment and Behavior, 11*(4), 483-510.

Dube, L., Renaghan, L.M., and Miller, J.M. (1994, February). Measuring customer satisfaction for strategic management. *The Cornell H.R.A. Quarterly,* 30-47.

Duke, C.R., and Persia, M.A. (1994). Foreign and domestic escorted tour expectations of American travelers. *Journal of International Consumer Marketing, 6*(3-4), 61-77.

Edgell, D.L. (1990). Trends in international tourism through the year 2000. *Trends, 27*(3),32-39.

Edgell, D.L. (1993). *World tourism at the millennium.* Washington, D.C.: U.S. Department of Commerce, U.S. Travel and Tourism Administration.

Egan, M. (1976). Interfaces between tourism and outdoor recreation. *Review of Tourism, 31*(2), 6-10.

Ethridge, F.M. (1982). A migration model of pleasure travel. *Sociological Spectrum, 2,* 99-121.

Fishbein, M., and Ajzen, I. (1975). *Belief, attitude, intention, and behavior.* Reading, MA: Addison-Wesley.

Fischer, E., and Farina, A. (1978). Attitude toward abortion and attitude-relevant overt behavior. *Social Forces, 57*(2), 585-599.

Fisk, R.P. (1981). Toward a consumption evaluation process model for services. In J.H. Donnelly and W.R. George, *Marketing of services*. Chicago: Marketing Association Proceeding Series.

Floyd, M. (1993a). Recreational Research Survey of Moores Creek National Battlefield. Final Report Submitted to the National Park Service, Texas A&M University. College Station.

Floyd, M. (1993b). *Recreational research survey of Cape Lookout National Seashore*. Final report submitted to the National Park Service, College Station, TX: Texas A&M University.

Fornell, C., Johnson, M.D., Anderson, E.W., Cha, J., and Bryant, B.E. (1996, October). The American customer satisfaction index: Nature, purpose, and findings. *Journal of Marketing, 60*, 7-18.

Francken, D.A., and van Raaij, W.F. (1981). Satisfaction with leisure time activities. *Journal of Leisure Research, 13*(4), 337-352.

Getty, J.M., and Thompson, K.N. (1994). A procedure for scaling perceptions of lodging quality. *Hospitality Research Journal, 18*(2), 75-96.

Glass, R.J., and More, T.A. (1992). Satisfaction, valuation, and views toward allocation of Vermont goose hunting opportunities. Research Paper NE-668, U.S.D.A. Forest Service.

Goodrich, J.N. (1977). Benefit bundle analysis: an empirical study of international travelers. *Journal of Travel Research, 16*(2),6-9.

Goodrich, J.N. (1978). The relationship between preferences for and perceptions of vacation destinations: Application of a choice model. *Journal of Travel Research, 17*(2), 8-13.

Griffin, A., and Hauser, J.R. (1992). *The voice of the customer* (Report No. 92-106). Cambridge, MA: Marketing Science Institute.

Griffin, J. (1995). *Customer loyalty*. New York: Lexington Books.

Guinn, R. (1980). Elderly recreational vehicle tourists: Life satisfaction correlates of leisure satisfaction. *Journal of Leisure Research, 12*(3),198-204.

Gunn, C.A. (1988). *Tourism planning*. New York: Taylor and Francis.

Gunn, C.A. (1990). Must tourism threaten parks? *Trends, 27*(3), 5-9.

Hammitt, W.E., McDonald, C.D., and Noe, F.P. (1984). Use level and encounters: Important variables of perceived crowding among nonspecialized recreationists. *Journal of Leisure Research, 16*(1),1-8.

Hanan, M., and Karp, P. (1989). *Customer satisfaction*. New York: Amacom.

Harris, L. (1992). [Poll]. *Travel and Leisure Magazine*.

Havitz, M.E., Dimanche, F., and Howard, D.R. (1993). A two-sample comparison of personal involvement inventory (PII) and involvement profile (IP) scales using selected recreation activities. *Journal of Applied Recreation Research, 17*(4), 331-364.

Heberlein, T., and Black, J.S. (1976). Attitude specificity and the prediction of behavior in a field setting. *Journal of Personality and Social Psychology, 33*(4), 474-479.

Herche, J. (1994). *Measuring social values: A multi-item adaptation to the list of values (MILOV)*.(Report No. 94-101). Cambridge, MA: Marketing Science Institute.

Herrick, T.A., and McDonald, C.D. (1992). Factors affecting overall satisfaction with a river recreation experience. *Environmental Management 16*(2), 243-247.

Heskett, J.L., Sasser, W.E., and Schlesinger, L.A. (1977). *The service profit chain.* New York: The Free Press.

Hill, A.V. (1992). *Field service management.* Homewood, IL: Business One Irwin.

Hinton, T., and Schaeffer, W. (1994). *Customer focused quality.* Englewood Cliffs, NJ: Prentice Hall.

Hughes, D.A. (1977). An investigation of the relation of selected factors to consumer socialization. In K.H. Hunt, *Conceptualization and measurement of consumer satisfaction and dissatisfaction.* (Report No. 77-103). Cambridge, MA: Marketing Science Institute.

Hull, R.B., Stewart, W.P., and Yi, Y.K. (1992). Experience patterns: Capturing the dynamic nature of a recreation experience. *Journal of Leisure Research, 24*(3), 240-252.

Hunt, K.H. (1977a). *Consumer satisfaction and dissatisfaction: Perspectives and overview.* (Report No. 77-112). Cambridge, MA: Marketing Science Institute.

Hunt, K.H. (1977b). *Conceptualization and measurement of consumer satisfaction and dissatisfaction.* (Report No. 77-103). Cambridge, MA: Marketing Science Institute.

Husbands, W. (1994). Vistor expectations of tourism benefits in Zambia. *Journal of International Consumer Marketing, 6*(3-4), 21-38.

Iso-Ahola, S.E. (1980). *The social psychology of leisure and recreation.* Dubuque, IA: William C. Brown.

Jurowski, C., Cumbow, M.W., Uysal, M., and Noe, F.P. (1995-6). The effects of instrumental and expressive factors on overall satisfaction in a park environment. *Journal of Environmental Systems, 24*(1), 47-67.

Jurowski, C., Uysal, M., and Noe, F.P. (1993). U.S. Virgin Islands National Park: A factor-cluster segmentation study. *Journal of Travel & Tourism Marketing, 1*(4), 3-31.

Jurowski, C., Uysal, M., Williams, D., and Noe, F.P. (1995). An examination of preferences and evaluations of visitors based on environmental attitudes: Biscayne Bay National Park. *Journal of Sustainable Tourism, 3*(2), 73-86.

Kabanoff, B. (1982). Occupational and sex differences in leisure needs and leisure satisfaction. *Journal of Occupational Behavior, 3*, 233-245.

Kahle, L, Klingel, D., and Kulka, R. (1981). Longitudinal study of adolescents: attitudes-behavior consistency. *Public Opinion Quaterly, 45*, 402-414.

Kahn, H. (1976). The Next 200 Years. New York: William Morrow

Kelly, H.L., Langenau, E.E., and Levine, R.L. (1990). Dimensions of hunting satisfaction: Multiple-satisfactions of wild turkey hunting. *Leisure Sciences, 12*(4), 383-393.

Kelly, J.R. (1981). Social benefits of outdoor recreation. *Forest Service Report*, U.S.D.A. Forest Service.

Kelly, J.R., Steinkamp, M.W., and Kelly, J.R. (1986). Later-life leisure: How they play in Peoria. *The Gerontologist, 26*, 531-537.

Kelly, J.R., Steinkamp, M.W., and Kelly, J.R. (1987). Later-life satisfaction: Does leisure contribute? *Leisure Sciences, 9*(3), 189-199.

Kirwin, P. (1992, October). Increasing sales and profits through guest satisfaction. *The Cornell H.R.A. Quarterly*, 38-9.

Krieger, M. (1973, February). What's wrong with plastic trees? *Science, 179*, 446-55.

Krishnan, H.S., and Olshavsky, R.W. (1995). The duel role of emotions in consumer satisfaction/dissatisfaction. *Advances in Consumer Research, 22*(XXII), 454-460.

Labone, M. (1996). The roaring silence in the sociology of leisure. *Social Alternatives, 15*(2), 30-32.

Labovitz, G., Chang, Y.S., and Rosansky, V. (1993). *Making quality work*. New York: Harper Business.

Ladki, S.M., and Nomani, M.Z.A. (1996). Consumer involvement in restaurant selection: A measure of satisfaction/dissatisfaction (part II). *Journal of Nutrition in Recipe & Menu Development, 2*(1), 15-32.

Larsson, L.M. (1994). *Perpetuating the South: Promotion between cultural boundaries*. International Sociological Association Paper.

Lawler, E.E. (1972). *Motivation in work organizations*. Monterey, CA: Brooks-Cole Publishing.

Leiper, N. (1990). Tourist attraction systems. *Annals of Tourism Research, 17*(3), 367-384.

Leiss, W. (1979). *The limits to satisfaction*. Canada: University of Toronto Press.

Lele, M.M., and Sheth, J.N. (1991). *The customer is key*. New York: John Wiley & Sons.

Levenstein, H.A. (1996, November 17). *Dripping with customer service*. The New York Times, 12.

Lewis, R.C., and Pizam, A. (1981, November). Guest surveys: A missed opportunity. *The Cornell, H.R.A. Quarterly*, 37-44.

Lieber, S.R., and Fesenmaier, D.R. (1985). Physical and social conditions affecting recreation site preferences. *Environment and Planning, 17*(12), 1613-1625.

Linder, S. (1970). *The harried leisure class*. New York: Columbia University Press.

Lounsbury, J.W., and Hoopes, L.L. (1985). An investigation of factors associated with vacation satisfaction. *Journal of Leisure Research, 17*(1), 1-13.

Lounsbury, J.W., and Polik, J.R. (1992). Leisure needs and vacation satisfaction. *Leisure Sciences, 14*(2), 105-119.

Lytle, J.F. (1993). What do your customers really want? Chicago: Probus Publishing.

Machlis, G., and Medlin, N.C. (no date). *Serving the visitor*. Moscow, ID: University of Idaho, Cooperative Park Studies Unit.

Maddox, R.N. (1985). Measuring satisfaction with tourism. *Journal of Travel Research, 23*(3), 2-5.

Mahfood, P.E. (1993). *Customer crisis.* Chicago: Probus Publishing.

Mahoney, E.D. (1987). Recreational marketing: The need for a new approach. *Visions in Leisure and Business, 5*(4), 53-71.

Mandell, M. (1989). Estimating the marketing effect of intervening variables in pooled cross-sectional and time series designs: Model specification and estimation procedure. *Evaluation Review, 13*(2), 174-200.

Mannell, R.C., and Iso-Ahola, S. E. (1987). Psychological nature of leisure and tourism experience. *Annals of Tourism Research, 14*(3), 314-33

Manning, R.E. (1985). *Studies in outdoor recreation.* Corvallis, OR: Oregon State University Press.

Manning, R.E., and Ciali, C.P. (1980). Recreation density and user satisfaction: A further exploration of the satisfaction model. *Journal of Leisure Research, 12*(4), 328-345.

McCartney, S. (1997, February 7). Vacations with Ringo, Elvis, and Cobain. *The Wall Street Journal,* B1.

McIntoch, R.W., Goeldner, C.R., and Ritchie, J.R. (1995). *Tourism.* New York: John Wiley & Sons.

Miller, J.A. (1977). Studying satisfaction, modifying models, eliciting expectations, posing problems and making meaningful measurements. In K.H. Hunt, *Conceptualizations and measurement of consumer satisfaction and dissatisfaction* (Report No. 77-193). Cambridge, MA: Marketing Science Institute.

Molm, L. (1991, August). Affect and social exchange: Satisfaction in power-dependence relations. *American Sociological Review, 56,* 475-93.

More, T.A., and Averill, J. (1992). *Satisfaction, happiness and emotion in the recreation experience: Are we asking the right questions?* The Fourth North American Symposium on Society and Resource Management, Madison, University of Wisconsin.

Naumann, E. (1995). Cincinnati, OH: Thomson Executive Press.

Neal, J.D., Sirgy, M.J., and Uysal, M. (1997). *The role of satisfaction with leisure travel/tourism services and experience in satisfaction with leisure life and overall life.* Manuscript submitted for publication.

Noe, F.P. (1987). Measurement specification and leisure satisfaction. Leisure Science. 9: 163-72.

Noe, F.P., and Hammitt, W.E. (1988). *Visual preferences.* Washington, D.C.: U.S. Government Printing Office.

O'Brien, R. (1977). *Marriott.* Salt Lake City, UT: Desert Book Company.

Oh, H., and Jeong, M. (1996). Improving marketers' predictive power of customer satisfaction on expectation-based target market levels. *Hospitality Research Journal, 19*(4), 65-85.

Oh, H., and Parks, S.C. (1997). Customer satisfaction and service quality: A critical review of the literature and service implications for the hospitality industry. *Hospitality Research Journal, 20*(3), 35-64.

Oliver, R.L., and Oliver, G.L. (1981). Effects of satisfaction and its antecedents on consumer preference and intention. In K.B. Monroe (Ed.), *Advances in consumer research*. Ann Arbor, MI: Association for Consumer Research.

O'Neill, M., Watson, H., and McKenna, M. (1994). Service quality in the Northern Ireland hospitality industry. *Managing Service Quality, 4*(3), 36-40.

Osgood, C.E., Suci, G.J., and Tannenbaum, P.H. (1957). *Measurement of meaning*. Urbana, IL: University of Illinois Press.

Parasuraman, A., Zeithaml, V.A., and Berry, L.L. (1984). A conceptual model of service quality and its implications for future research (Report No. 84-106). Cambridge, MA: Marketing Science Institute.

Parasuraman, A., Zeithaml, V.A., and Berry, L.L. (1994). *Moving forward in service quality research: Measuring different customer-expectation levels, comparing alternative scales, and examining the performance-behavioral intentions link* (Report No. 94-114). Cambridge, MA: Marketing Science Institute.

Patterson, P.G. (1993). Expectations and product performance as determinants of satisfaction for a high-involvement purchase. *Psychology & Marketing, 10*(5), 449-464.

Pizam, A. (1991). The management of quality tourism destinations. *AIEST 33*(St.-Gal Suisse), 79-87.

Pizam, A., and Milman, A. (1990). Current trends in manpower needs for the tourism industry. *Trends, 27*(3),14-17.

Pritchard, M.P., and Howard, D.R. (1997). The loyalty traveler: Examining a typology of service patronage. *Journal of Travel Research, 35*(4), 2-10.

Ragheb, M.G. (1979). *Age, sex, and their relationships to leisure satisfaction*: An exploratory study. Paper Presented at SPRE Research Symposium, National Recreation and Park Association, New Orleans, Louisiana.

Ragheb, M.G. (1980). Interrelationships among leisure participation, leisure satisfaction, and leisure attitudes. *Journal of Leisure Research, 12*(2), 138-49.

Ragheb, M.G., and Griffith, C. (1982). The contribution of leisure participation and leisure satisfaction to life satisfaction in older persons. *Journal of Leisure Research, 14*(4), 295-306.

Ragheb, M.G., and Tate, R.L. (1993). A behavioral model of leisure participation based on leisure attitude, motivation, and satisfaction. *Leisure Studies, 12*(1), 61-70.

Raucher, S.V. (1997a, January 26). Crowne Plaza hotel chain to unveil new TV ads. *The Atlanta Journal Constitution*, p. H8.

Raucher, S.V. (1997b, April 13). Hotel industry battles to keep its workers. *The Atlanta Journal Constitution*, p. R7.

Reichheld, F.F. (1996). *The loyalty effect*. Boston: Harvard Business School Press.

Riddick, C.C. (1986). Leisure satisfaction precursors. *Journal of Leisure Research, 18*(4), 259-65.

Riddick, C.C., and Stewart, D.G. (1994). An examination of the life satisfaction and importance of leisure in the lives of older female retirees: A comparison of blacks to whites. *Journal of Leisure Research, 26*(1), 75-87.

Robinson, J. (1973). Life satisfaction and happiness. In J. Robinson, and P.R. Shaver (Eds.), *Measures of social psychological attitudes*. Ann Arbor, MI: ISR.

Robinson, J., and Godbey, G. (1997). *Time for life*. State College, PA: Pennsylvania University Press.

Robinson, J., and Shaver, P.R. (1973). Measure of social psychological attitudes. Ann Arbor, MI: ISR.

Rokeach, H. (1968). *Beliefs, attitudes, and values*. San Francisco: Jossey-Bass.

Rollins, R.B. and Associates (1993). Managing the West Coast Trail. Strategic research & analysis section, *Parks Canada*.

Ross, G.F. (1993). Destination evaluation and vacation preference. *Annals of Tourism Research, 20*(3), 477-489.

Rossi, P., Freeman, H., and Wright, S. (1979). *Evaluation*. Beverly Hills, CA: Sage Publications.

Rutman, L. (1977). *Evaluation research methods: A basic guide*. Beverly Hills, CA: Sage Publications.

Ruyter, K., and Wetzels, M. (1997). On the perceived dynamics of retail service quality. *Journal of Retailing and Consumer Services, 4*(2), 83-88.

Ryan, C. (1995). *Researching tourist satisfaction*. New York: Routledge.

Saleh, F., and Ryan. C. (1991). Analyzing service quality in the hospitality industry using the SERVQUAL model. *Service Industries Journal, 11*(3), 324-45.

Sandifur, C.P. (1995). *Just give me real estate*. Spokane, WA: The Arthur H. Clark.

Schneider, B., and Bowen, D.E. (1995). *Winning the service game*. Boston: Harvard Business School Press.

Scitovsky, T. (1992). *The joyless economy*. Oxford, UK: Oxford University Press.

Seaton, A.V., and Tagg, S. (1995). The family vacation in Europe: Paedomorphic aspects of choices and satisfactions. *Journal of Travel & Tourism Marketing, 4*(1), 1-21.

Service, D. (1997). Disney University: No Mickey Mouse customer service. *Emory Report, 49*(19), 4.

Shelby, B. (1980). Crowding models for backcountry recreation. *Land Economics, 56*(1), 43-55.

Shelby, B., Lowney, D., and McKee, P. (1980). *Problems with satisfaction as a criterion for management and change*. Paper Presented at the Rural Sociological Society Meetings, Ithaca, New York.

Smith, S.L.J. (1994). The tourism product. *Annals of Tourism Research, 21*(3), 582-595.

Sneegas, J.J. (1986). Components of life satisfaction in middle and later life adults: Perceived social competence, leisure, participation, and leisure satisfaction. *Journal of Leisure Research, 18*(4), 248-58.

Snow, R.E. (1989). *Recreation resource management and planning study for the Biscayne National Park*. [Report]. Atlanta, GA: National Park Service Southeast Regional Office.

Sparks, B. (1994). Communicative aspects of the service encounter. *Hospitality Research Journal, 17*(2), 39-50.

Sparks, B., and Callan, V.J. (1996). Service breakdowns and service evaluations: The role of customer attributions. *Journal of Hospitality & Leisure Marketing, 4*(2), 3-24.

Spreng, R.A., Harrell, G.D., and Mackoy, R.D. (1995). Service recovery: Impact on satisfaction and intentions. *Journal of Services Marketing, 9*(1), 15-23.

Sun, L.H., and Uysal, M. (1994, Spring). The role of theme parks in tourism. *FIU Hospitality Review*, 71-80.

Survey Research Center, G.S.U. (1990a). *St. Augustine, Florida, visitor survey.* [Report]. Atlanta, GA: National Park Service, Southeast Regional Office.

Survey Research Center, G.S.U. (1990b).*Virgin Islands visitor survey.* [Report]. Atlanta, GA: National Park Service, Southeast Regional Office.

Swan, J., and Combs, L. (1976, April). Product performance and consumer satisfaction. *Journal of Marketing Research, 40*, 25-33

Swan, J., and Trawick, I.F. (1981). Automobile buyer satisfaction with the salesperson related to equity and disconfirmation. In H.K. Hunt and R.L. Day (Eds.), *Consumer satisfaction and complaining behavior.* Bloomington, IN: Indiana University Press.

Tan, A.L., and Kundrat, D. (1976). Values and modes of travel. *Perceptual and Motor Skills, 42*, 214.

Tate, U.S. (1984). Convergent and discriminant validity of measures of job, leisure, dyadic, and general life satisfaction by causal modeling methodology. *Journal of Leisure Research, 16*(3), 250-54.

Taylor, P.D., and Graefe, A.R. (no date). *Evaluating satisfaction in the river recreation experience in Big Bend National Park.* College Station, TX: The Texas A&M University, Texas Agricultural Extension Service.

Thurston, S. (1997, March 9). High expectations. *The Atlanta Journal Constitution*, p. D2.

Tinsley, H.A., Barrett,T.C., and Kass, R.A. (1977). Leisure activities and need satisfaction. *Journal of Leisure Research, 9*(2), 110-120.

Tinsley, H. A., and Kass, R.A. (1979). The latent structure of the need satisfying properties of leisure activities. *Journal of Leisure Research, 9*(4), 278-291.

Trafton, R.S., and Tinsley, H.A. (1980). An investigation of the construct validity of measures of job, leisure, dyadic and general life satisfaction. *Journal of Leisure Research, 12*(1), 34-44.

Tse, D., and Wilton, P. (1988, May). Models of consumer satisfaction formation: an extension. *Journal of Marketing, 25*, 204-212.

Ute, J. (1991). Travel behavior variation of overseas German visitors: Motivations, preferences, and activities. Unpublished thesis, Clemson University, South Carolina.

Uysal, M. (1998). The determinants of tourism demand: A theoretical perspective. In D. Ioannides and K. Debbage, *The economic geography of tourism.* London: Routlege.

Vaske, J.J., Donnelly, M.P., Heberlein, T.A., and Shelby, B. (1982). Differences in reported satisfaction ratings by consumptive and nonconsumptive recreationists. *Journal of Leisure Research, 14*(3),195-206.

Vaske, J., Donnelly, M.P., and Williamson, B.N. (1991). Monitoring for quality control in state park management. *Journal of Park and Recreation Administration, 9*(2), 59-72.

Vezina, R., and Nicosia, F.M. (1990). Investigations of the social determinants of consumer satisfaction and dissatisfaction. *Journal of Consumer Satisfaction and Dissatisfaction and Complaining Behavior, 3*, 36-41.

Volk, P. (1997, August 3). Entering hotel heaven. *The New York Times*, pp. 12, 14.

Walker, J.L. (1995). Service encounter satisfaction: conceptualized. *Journal of Services Marketing, 9*(1), 5-14.

Westbrook, R.A. (1980, June). Interpersonal affective influences on consumer satisfaction with products. *Journal of Consumer Research, 7*, 49-54.

Westbrook, R.A., and Oliver, R.L. (1981). Developing better measures of consumer satisfaction: Some preliminary results, In K.B. Monroe (Ed.), *Advances in consumer research*. Ann Arbor, MI: Association for Consumer Research.

Westbrook, R.A., and Reilly, M.D. (1983). Value percept disparity: An alternative to the disconfirmation of expectations theory of consumer satisfaction. In R.P Bagozzi and A.M. Tybout (Eds.), *Advances in consumer research*. Ann Arbor, MI: Association for Consumer Research.

Westflemish, P.B. (1974). Measuring attitudes for tourist marketing strategies. *Review of Tourism, 29*(3), 86-93.

Whipple, T.W., and Thach, S.V. (1988). Group tour management: Does good service produce satisfied customers? *Journal of Travel Research, 27*(2),16-21.

Wholey, J. (1977). Evaluability assessment. In L. Rutman (Ed.), *Evaluation research methods: A basic guide*. Beverly Hills, CA: Sage Publications.

Williams, D.R., and Patterson, M.E. (1991). Customer satisfaction with recreation sites: Evaluating a monitoring tool. Cooperative Research Report, No. 29-652. Blacksburg, VA: Virginia Polytechnic Institute and State University.

Withey, S.B. (1977). Integrating Some Models About Consumer Satisfaction. In K.H. Hunt, *Conceptualizations and measurement of consumer satisfaction and dissatisfaction* (Report No. 77-193). Cambridge, MA: Marketing Science Institute.

Wood, R.C. (1994). Hotel culture and social control. *Annals of Tourism Research, 21*(1), 65-80.

Wynne, R.J., and Groves, D.L. (1995). Life span approach to understanding coping styles of the elderly. *Education, 115*(3), 448-55.

Yi, Y.K. (1990). A Critical Review of Consumer Satisfaction. In V. Zeithaml (Ed.), *Review of marketing*. Chicago: American Marketing Association.

Zalatan, A. (1994). Tourist satisfaction: A predetermined model. *The Tourist Review, 1*, 9-13.

Zeithaml, V.A., Berry, L.L., and Parasuraman, A. (1987). *Communication and control processes in the delivery of service quality* (Report No. 87-100). Cambridge, MA: Marketing Science Institute.

■ Index